FAITH ENOUGH TO FINISH

FAITH ENOUGH to FINISH

JILL BRISCOE

TYNDALE HOUSE PUBLISHERS, INC. WHEATON, ILLINOIS

Visit Tyndale's exciting Web site at www.tyndale.com

Faith Enough to Finish

Copyright © 2001 by Jill Briscoe. All rights reserved.

Cover illustration copyright © 2001 by Debbie Hanley. All rights reserved.

Poems on pages vii–viii, 51, 180–181 by Jill P. Briscoe. All rights reserved.

Poem on page 161 copyright © 2001 by Jill P. Briscoe. All rights reserved.

Designed by Jenny Swanson

Edited by Susan Taylor and Linda Taylor

Published in association with the literary agency of Alive Communications, Inc., 7680 Goddard Street, Suite 200, Colorado Springs, CO 80920.

Unless otherwise indicated, all Scripture quotations are taken from the *Holy Bible*, New International Version®. NIV®. Copyright © 1973, 1978, 1984 by International Bible Society. Used by permission of Zondervan Publishing House. All rights reserved.

Scripture quotations marked NLT are taken from the *Holy Bible*, New Living Translation, copyright © 1996. Used by permission of Tyndale House Publishers, Inc., Wheaton, Illinois 60189. All rights reserved.

Scripture quotations marked KJV are taken from the *Holy Bible*, King James Version.

Scripture verses marked NEB are taken from *The New English Bible*, copyright © 1970, Oxford University Press, Cambridge University Press.

Library of Congress Cataloging-in-Publication Data

Briscoe, Jill.
   Faith enough to finish / by Jill Briscoe.
     p. cm.
   ISBN 0-8423-5310-0 (pbk.)
   1. Bible. O.T. Jeremiah—Criticism, interpretation, etc.   I. Title.
BS1525.2 .B75 2001
   224'.206—dc21   2001002385

Printed in the United States of America

07 06 05 04 03 02 01
7   6   5   4   3   2   1

To our children and their partners:
Dave and Rhea, Judy and Greg, and Peter and Libby,
who are our sheer delight, who challenge us
to go for God's gold, and whose lives demonstrate
a faith that works in an increasingly crazy
and unworkable world.

CHISELED

Those whom God crafts he chooses. Those he chooses he chisels. Like Michelangelo "seeing" his David in a lump of marble, God sees what he will make of us—finished and perfected according to his pattern. This doesn't happen, however, without a whole lot of chiseling!

Chiseled by the circumstances ministry arranges
Hammered by the things allowed that made such drastic changes
In my life and fondest dreams I'd hoped to realize,
Chiseled by my circumstance—I'm chiseled down to size!

Chiseled by the Word of God that happened to my heart
Shattered by the truth I know you want me to impart
Broken by the Word of power that had first broken me
Drawn by the fire of God to speak and set it free.

Chiseled by the people that you bring into my life
People who are difficult and cause me grief and strife.
Teach me, Lord, to honor them and help me, Lord, to see
They're not as near as awkward or as difficult as me.

Chiseled by my secret pride I choose not to confess
Sobered by your knowing that my life's so passionless
Shaped by all my sad regrets that cause you so much grief
Chiseled by my secret sin and shallow unbelief!

Chiseled by my children's choices—chiseled by their pain
Feeling I can hardly breathe or ever smile again!
Daring not to glance at Heaven and see my Father frown
Yet looking anyway, to see compassion smiling down.

So chisel on, Lord, till you see the likeness of your Son.
Blow by loving blow remake the image you've begun.
I only want to be like you so still me in your hands.
Lord, craft this piece of "marble me"
Into the pattern planned.

Jill P. Briscoe

CONTENTS

CHAPTER ONE
FAITH IN GOD'S FAITHFULNESS:
GOD IS GOD ENOUGH
1

CHAPTER TWO
FAITH FOR EVERY MOMENT:
HIS HOPE IN YOUR HEART
7

CHAPTER THREE
FAITH IN GOD'S PLAN:
HIS PLAN IN YOUR LIFE
25

CHAPTER FOUR
FAITH IN GOD'S CALL:
HIS WORK IN YOUR HAND
43

CHAPTER FIVE
FAITH IN GOD'S WORD:
HIS WORD IN YOUR MOUTH
63

CHAPTER SIX
FAITH IN GOD'S REFRESHMENT:
YOUR ROOTS IN HIS RIVER
87

CHAPTER SEVEN
FAITH TO HANDLE CONFLICT:
HIS MAN ON YOUR TEAM
107

CHAPTER EIGHT
FAITH WHEN YOU SUFFER:
HIS TEARS ON YOUR FACE
131

CHAPTER NINE
FAITH THAT PERSEVERES:
HIS STRENGTH FOR YOUR DAYS
153

CHAPTER TEN
FAITH ENOUGH TO FINISH:
I AM HEARD   175

OTHER BOOKS BY JILL BRISCOE   183

ABOUT THE AUTHOR   185

INTRODUCTION

FIRST, A NOTE OF THANKS TO MY MINISTRY ASSISTANT (AND daughter-in-law!), Rhea Briscoe, who encouraged me to "finish the work God gave me to do" and finish this book! She was my Baruch!

As you read this book, I hope you learn to appreciate, as I did, the faith walk of two of God's great servants, Jeremiah and his indomitable scribe, Baruch. As you study with me the books of Jeremiah and Lamentations, you will find that in some cases I did what I call "peeking around the corner of a verse." I tried to see who was standing in the shadows. I sought to get under the spiritual skin of these men and feel their joys and their pain. In other words, I needed to understand what gave them, against all odds, "faith enough to finish"!

Like Jeremiah and Baruch, I also want to finish strong. I want to know what it means to wake up every daily day, look at the sky, and whatever the weather, hit the day running for God. I want to make a difference. I want to change my world.

But my world doesn't want me to change it! It is spinning onward toward its climax, and who but the God who made it is able to halt its course, set it down, and talk some sense into it? This book comes out of my great desire to experience a faith that works with God toward that end. I find in the characters of Jeremiah and Baruch a sterling faith that laughs at the devil and says, "This can be done." I want to be like them when I grow up! I hope you do too.

Having faith enough to finish means having faith enough to start. Make sure that "by grace through faith" God is living in your heart. Then reach for the stars! See you when we get there!

Jill Briscoe

CHAPTER ONE

FAITH IN GOD'S FAITHFULNESS

※

GOD IS GOD ENOUGH

Because of the Lord's great love we
are not consumed, for his compassions
never fail. They are new every morning;
great is your faithfulness.
LAMENTATIONS 3:22-23

THE YEAR WAS 2000, AND I HAD ARRIVED AT THE AGE WHERE publishers were asking me to write books about the empty nest—what I would do differently as I looked back over a "long" life of ministry or what grandmothering has taught me!

I acknowledged the fact that I most certainly was looking back on more than I was looking forward to, but I still caught myself thinking, *When I grow up, I want to be* _____. Stuart shared the same wonder at our ages. Each birthday my husband would wake up and say something like, "How can someone as young as I am be as old as this?" He was seventy and I was sixty-five when God called us out of the pastorate as surely as he had called us in. It was November 12, 2000, and we were just about to start a whole new chapter of our ministry lives. After spending thirty years at Elmbrook Church, we were about to be commissioned as ministers-at-large and sent around the world on a new assignment.

"They must be crazy; they're workaholics; they can't let go," a few whisperers whispered. But all of our family and most of our friends, intercessors, and colleagues—and significantly, our beloved church family—were sweetly and thoroughly excited for us. For this we were humbly grateful. This was a new calling, you see. And those who had loved and supported us for three decades entered into a sweet sense of partnership with us. This was a new day and a new way of making full proof of our ministry. This moment started a new age on a new page of eternal history. My main concern is that we have faith enough to finish whatever chapters are left in the book of our lives—and to finish well—so that when God finally closes the book, others will be glad they have read it.

It was no coincidence that I was studying, teaching, and writing this book about the prophet Jeremiah and his friend Baruch at the time. We have little in common with this man, of course. We have not lived at the lowest point of our nation's history, offered babies as living sacrifices in our church, or known what it's like to have the most powerful nations on earth sack our city. Nor have we had the incredible personal trials and troubles this lover of God faced (though we have had our moments!).

We also know nothing about the punishing nonresponse to over forty years of preaching and prophesying that Jeremiah experienced. Instead, we have been blessed with generous and gratifying comments from those to whom and with whom we have ministered. But we do have the main thing in common with the weeping prophet, and that is the main thing! We share a common goal and the same intense desire to fulfill our primary calling to a relationship with God and our secondary calling to the task he has in mind for us—whatever the odds.

Married in 1958, Stuart and I are lifelong partners, together in heart and focus, united in body, soul, and mind. By the grace of God, we sleep at night as forgiven sinners. We are, at the end of the day, simply and only Jesus lovers and glory givers. We love each other irrevocably; we love our children and their spouses and our children's children until it hurts; we love Jesus to distraction. We are ever conscious of the fact that we've only just begun to plumb the depths of all of these great loves of our lives.

There is breadth, depth, and height to both God's mercy and grace in allowing us borrowed hours to go deeper and higher with God than we have ever been before. We have committed what's left of our numbered years to the ride.

And what has Jeremiah had to say to us two excited and thankful people at this point in our lives? Actually, God's words to me through his prophet have come from the prophet's lamentations! It may seem a little on the strange side to be finding my inspiration from the book of Lamentations. This choice of text, however, should surprise no one who knows me. My dear friends well know that I love a good lamentation! In fact, some of them might be tempted to think Jill Briscoe must believe that "a lament a day keeps the devil away!"

But first and foremost, I have been reminded through Jeremiah that God is God enough! That his loving-kindness never fails. That his mercies are new every morning, and great is his faithfulness! The context of the incredible words in Lamentations 3:22-23 is the lowest point of Jeremiah's life and ministry. He is watching the rape of Jerusalem and the end of all his wildest dreams. Yet he is saying to all of us, "God is God enough!"

"But Jill," you may say, "God is God enough for what?"

And I answer, "Not for *what* but rather for *whom!*" That one is easy to answer: God is God enough for Jill Briscoe. Stuart and I can reaffirm, as we did on November 12, 2000, that God has been, is, and will be all that we need him to be when we need him to be all that we need! Whatever and wherever we are at any given moment of any given day, God is God enough! Morning by morning his mercy, love, and grace are ours.

And who better than God to know what we need? After all, he knew us before we knew us! And he chose us before we ever came to be. Because God has never had a thought he hasn't always had, we have always been heavy on his mind. Do you know how overwhelmingly grateful I am for that? God said to Jeremiah, "Before I formed you in the womb I knew you, before you were born I set you apart" (Jeremiah 1:5). God called Jeremiah first and foremost to himself.

I know also that I am shaped by the same heavenly Potter who shaped Jeremiah's life. I am hand painted with the colors of my culture. If you search for the trademark, you will find "Made in England" indelibly written somewhere on this woman's soul. The

English girl who lives inside this body thanks God for a wonderful English sister, red buses, high tea, roses, and a heritage of Churchill, the battle of Britain, Beatrix Potter, C. S. Lewis, Cambridge, Wordsworth, and his hosts of golden daffodils. I've been a long time away from my homeland, but then Jesus understands. It's just a few years shy of the years he spent away from his homeland (heaven) for me.

Like Jeremiah, I have not only been created, called, commissioned, and sent to another culture, but also God has shown me the work he had for me to do. What mercy; what grace! God put his plan in my life, his work in my hands, and his words in my mouth. He said to me as he said to Jeremiah, "I have put my words in your mouth" (Jeremiah 1:9) and added, "Tell them everything I command you; do not omit a word" (Jeremiah 26:2). And now it seems that he is saying it again!

Like Jeremiah, I have so often said, "I cannot do it. I cannot speak, I am a child." Many years ago I even wrote a book about my struggles in this regard called *Here am I; Send Aaron!* My excuses have been a little different from the excuses Moses or Jeremiah gave. In those days I would use the "I'm too young" excuse. A little later, I tried the "I'm too married" excuse, the "I'm too woman" excuse, and the "I'm too middle-aged" excuse. Lately, as you can imagine, I've been very tempted to voice the "I'm too tired" excuse and, of course, the "I'm too old" excuse!

But God has said to me in the depths of my soul, "*I am God enough! I am God enough for all of your excuses!*" And he has told me, as he told his prophet, to just do it and go on doing it until he tells me to stop. He has told me to do it for him and to do it with fire in my bones. So day by day by day I have told him what he already knows: I'll do it, and do it again and again in his daily strength and power because I love him.

There's quite enough mercy, quite enough compassion, and quite enough loving-kindness to go around. God is God enough, God is kind enough, God is good enough, and above all, God is love enough for the whole wide world. That includes you, me, and every-body else!

The faith God will give us to finish is the same faith he gave us to start this incredible adventure, this laughing life, this miracle of moments that has been touched with the Spirit's fragrance like wet grass shining after rain. He will turn laments into laughter and sorrow into shouts of triumph. You'll see, for he never changes, and great indeed is his faithfulness!

CHAPTER TWO

FAITH FOR EVERY MOMENT

HIS HOPE IN YOUR HEART

The Lord is good to those whose
hope is in him, to the one who seeks him.
LAMENTATIONS 3:25

ARE YOU A MORNING PERSON? I'M NOT. I CAN STAY THE
course at night, but I am a bear in the morning. But I am a Christian,
so in another way I *am* a morning person! In fact, I am a "morning
by morning" person! If we don't find the morning-by-morning way
to live the Christian life, our faith will not survive. We will never
find faith enough to finish. Faith that works is a faith for every
moment of every daily day.

The faith I experienced to trust God yesterday when my father
died may desert me today when my child gets sick. The trust I was
able to model to my children when I received some ominous medical news can fly out the window when my daughter goes out on her
first date! Why is it that the faith that worked yesterday may not
work today? Is it God's fault or mine? Well, it's not God's fault, so
it must be mine!

God is faithful all the time. I am faithful some of the time. God is
good all the time. I am good occasionally. God is full of compassion
all of the time. I can get a twinge of compassion on Thanksgiving or
when the Salvation Army rings their bells at Christmas. I am good at
exhibiting mercy to people who have hurt others but bad at offering
the same mercy to someone who has hurt me! So it is obvious that I
am not God! The problem is that I am me, but people expect me to
be like God—loving, good, compassionate, and merciful all the
time.

To be more like God and less like me, I need to stay close to him. The secret of faith for every moment is that I seek him out morning by morning, evening by evening, day by day. The more I make sure he is my constant companion, the more godly, or God-like, I will become. Isaiah affirms this when he talks about the reign of a righteous king, for during the reign of such a king, "each man will be like a shelter from the wind and a refuge from the storm, like streams of water in the desert and the shadow of a great rock in a thirsty land" (Isaiah 32:2). Because the King of kings reigns in my heart and life, I will become more like him day by day. I like to think of myself as the "shadow of a great rock"; that is, the shadow of *the* Rock, my Lord. As I determine to abide so close to the Rock that I am his constant shadow, then moment by moment and day by day I will become more like him, reflecting his mercy, compassion, and love.

As we study the prophet Jeremiah, we will see that he was God's constant companion. Jeremiah wept with compassion because he loved his people, and he was faithful to them and to God through thick and thin. And there was plenty of thick and thin in Jeremiah's life! He wrote of great faith in God even as he struggled, feared, and watched the destruction of his beloved city of Jerusalem.

The verse at the beginning of this chapter, Lamentations 3:25, is a magnificent statement of faith. The context of this statement, however, comes as Jeremiah wrote of the sack of Jerusalem. He wrote of a siege so horrific that minds would refuse to even take it in. Listen to the horror Jeremiah experienced: "My eyes fail from weeping, I am in torment within, my heart is poured out on the ground because my people are destroyed, because children and infants faint in the streets of the city. They say to their mothers, 'Where is bread and wine?' as they faint like wounded men in the streets of the city, as their lives ebb away in their mothers' arms" (Lamentations 2:11-12).

Many of us can identify with Jeremiah, who was subjected to an overdose of trouble. "I am the man who has seen affliction," he writes in Lamentations 3:1. Those words are probably the understatement of the book! He was a man who knew what it felt like to have his own family plot to kill him, his own church make him a laughingstock, and his one and only colleague regret he had ever met him. His leaders lowered him into a pit, where he sank up to his neck in mud, and then dropped stones on his head (Lamentations 3:52-53).

How does someone survive such excessive abuse? What happens to a person's belief system under such duress? What can you do when you are faced with such distress that your faith becomes shaky? Maybe you are watching the destruction of your highest hopes and fondest dreams, just as Jeremiah watched the destruction of Jerusalem. You need a faith that works in the face of overwhelming trouble. Perhaps you experienced faith in the face of adversity yesterday and yet find yourself struggling with faith enough for today. Moment by moment, morning by morning, God desires to supply you with faith enough to finish.

Morning by morning, crisis by crisis, day by day, Jeremiah learned to draw on the faithful God who loved him and provided for him. Morning by morning God's grace was sufficient; morning by morning God's mercy sustained him. The same can be true for us today. The compassionate God finds a way to cradle a person's dying faith in his arms and nurse it back to life. God is God enough!

We too need to experience God's grace morning by morning. That grace is available to us by faith through prayer. Prayer makes it possible for limited people to meet an unlimited God. As we deepen our relationship with God through prayer, as we remain as "shadows" to him, our Rock, we will discover faith that works—as Jeremiah did.

FAITH DISTRESS

Our concept of God can take such a hammering in adversity that our faith faints and prayer becomes impossible. We may not know it, but at that point we are suffering *faith distress*. What does faith distress feel like? It feels horrible! We don't feel like trusting God anymore because God does not appear to be the loving, kind, and merciful God we have always believed him to be. This is bound to leave us extremely insecure. There are several signs of faith distress.

Getting God and Life Mixed Up

One symptom of faith distress is the tendency to get God and life all mixed up: We blame God for all the evil we see or experience in life. In an illogical thought progression, we see cruelty in the world, we find ourselves thinking about the apparent cruelty of God, and then wrongly conclude that God is cruel. God is not cruel, however; *life* is cruel.

Have you ever done that? Jeremiah did. He described God as being like a bear who has mangled him and left him half dead by the side of the road: "He dragged me from the path and mangled me and left me without help" (Lamentations 3:11). "Life is a bear," he may have said in our modern vernacular. "God is attacking me." Jeremiah had God and life mixed up.

There is no doubt that Jeremiah had been mangled and mauled. Like Job, Jeremiah complained bitterly that he wished he were dead. But it was his relatives and friends who had waited like fierce animals to pounce on him and destroy him, not the Almighty.

In fact, God had warned Jeremiah that this was the case. "Beware of your friends; do not trust your brothers. For every brother is a deceiver, and every friend a slanderer. Friend deceives friend, and no one speaks the truth" (Jeremiah 9:4-5). Again the Lord spoke to his distraught prophet, "Your brothers, your own family—even they have betrayed you; they have raised a loud cry against you. Do not trust them, though they speak well of you" (Jeremiah 12:6). It was his own people at home in Anathoth who had turned their hands against Jeremiah again and again, yet he asserts in this lament, "Indeed, [God] has turned his hand against me again and again" (Lamentations 3:3).

Jeremiah complains further, "He has besieged me and surrounded me with bitterness and hardship" (Lamentations 3:5), yet it was the leaders of Israel who had put him under house arrest and worse. Jeremiah continues, "My splendor is gone and all that I had hoped from the Lord" (Lamentations 3:18). It was not God who had robbed him of his dreams but evil people. When you get God and life all mixed up, you confuse the source of the trouble with the only One who can truly help.

Extreme affliction does something to the mind, causing it to lose perspective on the whole situation. "I remember my affliction and my wandering," the prophet cries, "the bitterness and the gall. I well remember them, and my soul is downcast within me" (Lamentations 3:19-20). Jeremiah was busy remembering all the bad things that had happened to him, blaming God, and it caused him to be "downcast."

Have you ever pushed the "replay button" in your mind, going over and over the things that have happened to you until you are so depressed you want to die? If you have, you are not alone. It is very difficult not to revisit trouble in your mind, but it is not impossible. Jeremiah needed to realize that it was not God who had used him for target practice but the priests in Anathoth. It was not God who thought Jeremiah was a big joke; it was Jeremiah's own people. It was not God who had manhandled him but the temple police.

Similarly, you must realize that it was not God who walked out on you, it was your spouse. It was not God who took advantage of you at the office but your workmate. It was not God who was driving the car that killed your child but a drunken driver. We must not get God and life mixed up. Like Jeremiah, you may need to sit your soul down, give it a good talking to, and make it listen! David did that. He had to sit his soul down and give it a good talking to: "Why are you downcast, O my soul? Why so disturbed within me? Put your hope in God, for I will yet praise him, my Savior and my God. My soul is downcast within me; therefore I will remember you" (Psalm 42:5-6).

I remember getting God and life mixed up. One time my father lent his car showroom to an ex-prisoner of war for an art exhibit. The man had spent four grueling years in a Nazi prisoner-of-war camp. He was an artist by trade and managed to sketch the horrors inside the camp, hoping one day the world would see what had taken place. I was fifteen at the time and volunteered to help put up the exhibit.

I will never forget those horrific, graphic pictures. I thought, *Aren't the Jews God's people? What sort of God is he to allow such things to happen to his own? How cruel!* But it was not God's inhumanity that was painted in those sketches, it was man's. It was not God who had mangled their bodies, it was the soldiers. It was not God who carted the Jews off to the terrible death camps, it was the Germans under Hitler. It was not God who threw their bodies in a pit and dropped stones on their heads, it was their torturers. I had God and life mixed up. I needed to rethink my understanding of human evil and of God if I was ever to make any sense out of life.

How will you know whether your faith is in distress? Faith distress has telltale symptoms. The first is getting God and life mixed up. The second has to do with your prayer life.

Struggling in Your Prayer Life
When affliction comes and your faith becomes distressed, you may find that your prayer life takes a body blow! At times mine certainly has. As we listen to ourselves pray, we may hear ourselves praying like unbelievers. We may well find ourselves praying angry prayers, complaining prayers, bargaining prayers, accusing prayers. Just read Lamentations 3.

In his lamentations to God, Jeremiah accuses God of turning the lights off on him. "He has driven me away and made me walk in darkness rather than light" (Lamentations 3:2). He complains that God has put his hands over his ears and "even when I call out or cry for help, he shuts out my prayer" (Lamentations 3:8).

Jeremiah feels as if he has been used for target practice: "He drew his bow and made me the target for his arrows" (Lamentations 3:12). He wails, "He has broken my teeth with gravel" (Lamentations 3:16). Try listening to your prayers; they may tell you if you are experiencing faith distress!

One day I received a phone call that put me into a tailspin. My daughter-in-law had left her husband, my son. I fell to my knees. I remember my heart rate escalating. "Lord," I prayed. . . . Then my prayer turned into garbled words. I couldn't believe I was praying like this! Had I learned nothing in over forty years of knowing Christ and serving him? I listened to myself charging God with sleeping on the job! I heard myself getting God and life mixed up, accusing him of behavior that had nothing whatsoever to do with him. Suddenly I didn't want to talk about it anymore. Not with him. My prayer life moved into a holding pattern!

In faith distress, you may find yourself unable or unwilling to pray. God understands. He knows your pain. Pray anyway, and tell him exactly how you feel. Those feelings are coming from your inner turmoil, another sign of faith distress.

Facing Inner Turmoil

Jeremiah knew about inner turmoil. "I have been deprived of peace," the prophet records in Lamentations 3:17. Peace is not a fuzzy feeling. Peace is, as Augustine put it, "the tranquility of order." When my spirit is out of order and I am falling apart on the inside and blaming God for it, I am probably suffering a bad case of faith distress. There is an uneasy awareness that things are not the way they ought to be. My world is seriously out of sync, and I feel a real resentment toward God. *It is his fault*, we tell ourselves. *This trouble happened on his watch. He is the robber; I am the robbed.*

A friend of mine had been sexually abused when she was a small child. As she struggled to make sense of what God had allowed to happen to her, she got God and life mixed up and ended up in a great state of spiritual confusion.

"What is your concept of God?" I asked her.

"At first," she replied, "I found it difficult to believe that he even existed. But I knew that was silly because I knew he did. Then I really had a problem! It was easier to believe that he *wasn't* there than that he *was!* If he was, how could he stand by in a corner of the room with his hands in his pockets? What sort of a God is he? How could he do this to me?"

But it wasn't God who had abused her; it was her father. And God had delivered her out of the situation in a remarkable way. God was not the robber.

When you face such inner turmoil, you need to talk to God about it, for ultimately only he can make sense of it. Only he can restore your faith.

Lacking Direction

The next symptom of faith distress is a lack of direction in life, confusion as to which way to go or what decision to make. Jeremiah attributed his confusion to God: "He has barred my way with blocks of stone; he has made my paths crooked" (Lamentations 3:9).

I can remember thinking that God was playing a game with me by sending me up a road and then going on ahead of me and turning all the signposts around just to confuse me! That is not a good feeling!

We were trying to discern whether to come to America to live. We received an invitation to immigrate and started up the road in that direction. Then all sorts of roadblocks appeared in our way. I became confused. Why would God call us to America and then put roadblocks in our way? I began to suffer faith distress.

But it wasn't God who was blocking our way. It was immigration, red tape, and government departments on both sides of the Atlantic. As soon as I applied my faith in the faithfulness of God, the way became clear again and the roadblocks disappeared.

Your faith can be distressed when you feel confused and don't know what to do. Never forget that God is not out to confuse you—he will eventually make the path clear. Be patient and remain faithful.

Feeling Disappointed with God

Another telltale symptom of faith distress is feeling disappointment with God. This might be a horrible sense of betrayal, much like what Jeremiah felt: "My splendor is gone and all that I had hoped from the Lord" (Lamentations 3:18). Jeremiah felt that God had let him down—badly. All his hopes and dreams—personal hopes, political hopes, prophetic hopes—lay buried under the rubble that had been the holy city of Jerusalem.

Have you ever felt that all your hopes and dreams lie under the rubble of a divorce, job loss, or child problems? Perhaps it is your faith that lies in ruins, and you feel betrayed by the very God who promised you so much. Like Jeremiah you complain, "All that I had hoped from the Lord is gone."

Stuart and I had given up our careers to cast our lot with a work

among teenagers. After we arrived at a Christian ꜀
things did not turn out quite the way I expected. I f꜀
thought that God had let us in for a disappointment.
was unfair and unjust. All I had hoped from the Lorᵈ

But this was most unfair and unjust of me. We had mistaken the
job description we had been given. It was no one's fault, certainly
not God's! Once I began to unmix God and life, this period of our
lives became a perfect opportunity to develop our faith.

FAITH DEVELOPMENT

The first step to renewing your faith at the low points of your life is
to recognize the symptoms of faith distress. The second step is to
take charge of your spiritual life and realize that the conditions you
are living in are ideal for God to develop your faith.

This process has two sides to it. I am responsible for "mind
work," and God is responsible for "heart work." (Of course, I
understand that God also does work on our minds as we learn from
his Word and pray for his guidance, but that's not what I'm talking
about here.)

Listen to Jeremiah as he does his mind work: "I remember my affliction and my wandering, the bitterness and the gall. I well remember them, and my soul is downcast within me. Yet this I call to mind
and therefore I have hope" (Lamentations 3:19-21). How do we do
this mind work? By taking responsibility for what we "call to mind."

I can remember discovering this principle early in my Christian
faith. The truth that I could do something about my thinking was a
huge step in my own faith development. I did not need to be a vic-
tim of my own negative thinking or of the thoughts that the devil
planted in my fertile imaginings. I could take charge of my own
thought patterns.

My part was to select the right channel and to choose the right
tape. I could truly be selective in what I drew out of my memory
bank. I could constantly call bad memories to mind, and the result
would be despondency or worse. Or I could call good things to
mind, and the result would be renewed faith and hope.

There is a good example of this in Lamentations 3: "Those who were my enemies without cause hunted me like a bird. They tried to end my life in a pit and threw stones at me; the waters closed over my head, and I thought I was about to be cut off" (vv. 52-54). Notice how Jeremiah minds his mind and corrals his thoughts. Instead of dwelling on the nightmare of drowning in mud while rocks were dropped on his head, he "calls to mind" his desperate cry for help and what happened next: "I called on your name, O Lord, from the depths of the pit. You heard my plea: 'Do not close your ears to my cry for relief.' You came near when I called you, and you said, 'Do not fear.' O Lord, you took up my case; you redeemed my life" (vv. 55-58).

When you are in the pit with people throwing stones at you, don't think about the stones; think about how God will help you out of it by remembering how he has helped you in the past! Jeremiah focused his thoughts on how God got right down in the pit with him. He remembered how God had delivered him before. Jeremiah minded his mind, and God minded his heart!

When I am in a pit, I have learned to use my mind to remember an answered prayer. This is one reason I keep a prayer diary, because in the heat of the moment I don't always have a good memory. It is good to have recorded incidents in my life when God has answered specific prayers for my children. When they are in urgent need of prayer again, it helps to turn in that record to past incidents and be reminded of answered prayer. That gives me hope to pray, "Do it again, Lord!"

After you have thought about how God has helped you in trouble, don't stop. It's tempting to start thinking about the trouble again at once. Think about God. Think about his character. That's what Jeremiah did.

"Because of the Lord's great love we are not consumed, for his compassions never fail. They are new every morning; great is your faithfulness" (Lamentations 3:22-23).

God is a consuming fire, but because of his love he will not consume us. God is a forgiving God, full of mercy and grace. This will never change! People will change, circumstances will change, but God will never change! Great is his faithfulness! He is faithful to us even when we are not faithful to him. Practicing remembering these positive things about the Lord will start to develop our faith muscles. So faith development means starting with mind work and then cooperating with the Lord as he begins his heart work in you. How do we cooperate with him in our faith development? Jeremiah tells us the steps.

Tell Yourself the Truth

"I say to myself, 'The Lord is my portion; therefore I will wait for him' " (Lamentations 3:24). Jeremiah is telling himself the truth. "The Lord is all I have," he says. "The Lord is also my future, my inheritance. He is all I have now and all I will have in the future."

If God is the sum total of all you care about, then it makes perfect sense to spend time in his company, deliberately putting yourself in his presence as often as you can. Of course, you need to decide if this is, indeed, the truth about yourself. Perhaps the Lord is not the sum total of your life. If he is not, start there, and make a decision about that. If you want him to be the focal point of all you are and do, you can tell him so right now. If you want him to take care of your past by his forgiving mercies, fill your present with his presence, and be the sum total of your future, then convey that to him in words. Be truthful with yourself.

Put Yourself into Silence

"Let him sit alone in silence, for the Lord has laid it on him" (Lamentations 3:28). Start a habit of sitting in silence until you become conscious that you are not alone. God's waiting room is a grand place to be! You will need to find a solitary place. As I have worked hard at this, I have discovered that hope is more often birthed in silence than in noise.

Many people find it hard to cope with quiet, yet quiet helps us to cope! A relative of mine used to fill his environment with sound. I came to realize he didn't want to be alone. It made him uncomfortable. He didn't want to hear the still small voice of conscience. Our postmodern contemporary Christian world needs to rediscover the use of silence and not be afraid of it.

Find a time, and find a place. Get up early, and get up regularly in order to meet with God. Remember that sleep deprivation is better than God deprivation. Pay the price necessary to achieve the disciplines required to discover him in the garden of your soul. You will never be sorry!

Stay Until You Sense His Grace

"It is good to wait quietly for the salvation of the Lord" (Lamentations 3:26). Quietness is soul therapy. *Staying* in the quiet of God's presence brings tranquility back to a frantic spirit.

Staying in quietness is a foreign concept in our industrialized society. The psalmist said that the Shepherd of our souls would lead his sheep beside "quiet waters" (Psalm 23:2). Zephaniah promised that God will "quiet you with his love" (Zephaniah 3:17). Isaiah affirmed that "in quietness and trust is your strength" (Isaiah 30:15), later saying that "the effect of righteousness will be quietness and confidence forever" (32:17).

The spiritual concepts of nourishment, satisfaction, strength, and confidence will be realized in "quietness."

What are you needing God to do for you right now? Perhaps you are hungry or thirsty for his grace, love, or power. Perhaps you need rest from a guilty conscience. Maybe you need forgiveness. Perhaps you need strength to face a difficult situation, and confidence to trust in God. Stay with God until you sense his gracious response to your need.

Forgive Yourself

Think about standing before God. Listen to your words. You might say something like, "O Lord, do you remember that awful thing I did?" If you do, you will hear him reply, "No. What thing?" As God said to Jeremiah, "I will forgive their wickedness and will remember their sins no more" (Jeremiah 31:34).

When I first became a Christian, I had trouble believing that I was forgiven. It was hard for me to believe that God had forgotten what I couldn't help but remember. God had forgiven me, but I couldn't forgive myself.

It was a long time before I could trust what the Bible said about the forgiveness of God. What love and patience it took for him to show me such mercy and grace.

I realized that one day every human being will stand before God. To each one he will say either, "I forgive you" or "I forget you." There is no middle ground, no partial forgiveness. God has forgiven you completely. Those who learn how much they have been forgiven can also know that they will never be forgotten.

The problem is staying still enough and silent enough long enough to allow God the chance to do his renewing work. Staying still until the focus of your heart shifts from you to him takes tenacity and discipline. The effort, however, is so worthwhile! You will know when that takes place. You will stop thinking about yourself. What a novel thought!

I never realized how self-centered I was until I began to practice being still and quiet. There I was, filling the center of my thinking. I couldn't escape from my horrible self-absorption. I was everywhere. I found that if I asked God to help me to change my self-absorption to God-absorption and sat there long enough for him to do that renewing work within me, it actually began to happen!

If I waited stubbornly and patiently, but with confidence, until his work was done in me and for me, I found that he recreated spiritual life and perspective in my heart. It is good to wait with quietness and confidence for the good being done in you and through you. When you have truly experienced God's forgiveness yourself, then you are ready for God to take your faith and display it to the world.

FAITH DISPLAYED

Faith distress can lead us to faith development so that our faith is displayed to the world. Jeremiah's words in Lamentations reveal three qualities of genuine faith displayed to the world. And all three of them have to do with our attitudes.

Genuine Faith Believes in God's Goodness

"The Lord is good to those whose hope is in him, to the one who seeks him," we read in Lamentations 3:25.

I had some friends who lost a child in an accident. They moved into a "faith distress" mode. Then they allowed God to develop their faith in him in the crisis. As the parents rushed to the hospital, one prayed out loud, "Oh, God, will you be good to us and save our child?" The other parent said, "There's something wrong with that prayer. Isn't God good if the boy dies?"

Together they came to the realization that God was good whether the child lived or not! Bad things that happen do not change the character of God! The child did, in fact, pass away, but my friends displayed a faith in the goodness of God despite the bad outcome of the incident.

Unwavering faith in God's goodness is a display of faith that amazes the world and brings great glory to God.

Genuine Faith Stops Whining

The thing that impressed me about my friends was their refusal to complain. They refused to complain about the hospital, the paramedics, or the endless red tape once they arrived at the hospital. They didn't complain about the expense of the funeral or the inappropriate remarks of people who offered glib comments on things they really didn't understand. They cheerfully persevered in their ongoing ministry, not without appropriate tears, but with a stubborn affirmation in God's sovereign goodness. In other words, they refused to whine!

What are you busy whining about at the moment? In our son and daughter-in-law's kitchen, they have put up a plaque for their seven children. It simply says: No Whining! God wants us to put one of those up on the wall of our minds, too.

None of us likes to suffer in silence. We like to lament loudly!

Sometimes I think Christians are the world's worst whiners! Why is it that believers so often portray such a piqued attitude? It is as if we feel we have an inalienable right to a charmed life! God wants us to stop whining when we face difficulty. Instead, he wants us to humbly submit to the difficulty and bear it patiently, knowing that he has permitted the situation.

Jeremiah wrote of a man who should "bury his face in the dust" (Lamentations 3:29). He used this familiar picture of a person submitting himself to another by falling prostrate in the dirt in complete submission.

The aspect of humble submission has been incredibly hard for me. I just love to gripe and complain. It just comes naturally. And that is the problem, of course. It comes naturally. It is part of our sinful nature. We can monitor our growth in grace by our willingness to stop it.

God hates whiners! He was constantly telling the children of Israel to stop it. In fact, he is still telling us in the New Testament how he felt about all the grumbling his people did in the Old Testament: "Do not grumble, as some of [the Israelites] did—and were killed by the destroying angel" (1 Corinthians 10:10). If the destroying angel meted out such drastic punishment to whiners today, I wonder how many of us would be left?

The spirit of humble submission to hardship will display a faith that is working in a Christian's life.

Genuine Faith Cheerfully Perseveres

Scripture tells us, "Weeping may remain for a night, but rejoicing comes in the morning" (Psalm 30:5). We cannot grow spiritually until we exhibit a healthy faith that our troubled night will not last forever. Lamentations 3:31 says that "men are not cast off by the Lord forever."

As we wait out the storms of life, will we assert that God's compassion and mercy will come to our aid and that our loving God will not "willingly bring affliction" (Lamentations 3:33)? Will we speak up for him instead of speaking against him? Will we say loudly and clearly that we believe he is fully aware of our suffering and the injustice done to us and that nothing escapes his notice?

Above all, will we be willing to accept hardship and testing, knowing that they strengthen our faith? If our answer to that question is, "I will, the Lord helping me," then we are well on the way to experiencing a faith that works morning by morning for every moment of our days!

I suppose it comes down to a new willingness to be broken by the circumstances of life that God in his sovereign grace permits. When you do that, your faith distress becomes faith developed, which can then be gloriously displayed by God to a hungry world. You can have faith in the loving compassion of a merciful God, who will, moment by moment and crisis by crisis, supply all the grace you need.

"Though he brings grief, he will show compassion, so great is his unfailing love" (Lamentations 3:32).

TIME OUT

These worksheets can be used in groups, in church classes, or with individuals as a discipling tool. They can also be used in a personal quiet time.

Take Time

1. Discuss the symptoms of faith distress. Do you recognize any of these in your own life?

   • Getting God and life mixed up
   • Failing in your prayer life
   • Facing inner turmoil
   • Lacking direction
   • Feeling disappointed with God

2. Read Lamentations 3:1-33. Then take the symptoms listed above and match them to a verse (or verses) in this passage. (For example, "He has trampled me in the dust" in 3:16 would match "Getting God and life mixed up.")

3. Discuss this sentence: "I am responsible for 'mind work,' and God is responsible for 'heart work.'"

4. Which of the following elements do you struggle with and why?

   • Telling yourself the truth
   • Being "silent"
   • Staying until you sense his grace
   • Forgiving yourself

5. Read Lamentations 3:19-33. Match each verse to one of the following:

   • Belief in God's goodness
   • Willingness to stop whining
   • Cheerful perseverance

6. Which of the items listed in question 5 are you working on at the present time? Share your progress with the group.

Prayer Time
1. Praise God for being God enough in your life.
2. Pray for those who are struggling with their concept of God.
3. Pray Lamentations 3:23-24 for those you know who are facing difficulty.
4. Pray for yourself.
5. Pray for people who are struggling to persevere.

A Letter to God
Write a letter to God about your needs for his grace and mercy in your life. Ask him to help you discover faith morning by morning.

Good Morning Jesus!
Father Please take away any thoughts that don't glorify you. Keep me close to You today. I give my children & Grand Children to you, Keep them safe & Pure. Bless my husband.
I trust you & love you, Please help me with my unbelief.
Let me love you today with all my heart.
I love you! Sally

CHAPTER THREE

FAITH IN GOD'S PLAN

HIS PLAN IN YOUR LIFE

Before I formed you in the womb I knew you,
before you were born I set you apart.
JEREMIAH 1:5

I DID NOT EXPERIENCE FAITH THAT WORKS UNTIL I UNDER-stood that God had a plan for my life. Not just a general plan—to help me finish school, get a job, marry the man of my dreams, and have kids—but a specific plan. A plan that he planned for me before I was even conceived.

I understood that my parents had a plan for my life. They carefully planned for my schooling. They did the very best they could in postwar Britain to be thinking ahead and saving for my education.

Once I got to school, it didn't take long to figure out that my teachers had a plan for my life. They planned that I should graduate! As I got involved with sports and discovered that I had moderate talent, I won a coaching scholarship. There was no doubt about my trainer's purpose. He planned to turn me into a first-class tennis player. As soon as I was old enough to date, I found out that the boys I dated all had plans for my life! It seemed the whole world had plans for my life!

The idea that God also had a plan and that his was the master plan for my life never occurred to me. Unlike my parents, teachers, tennis coach, and boyfriends, I couldn't see God, didn't know him, and was not remotely interested in him or his plans. I had absolutely no idea that God had any personal interest in me at all. I considered it responsible behavior to take charge of my own affairs. I was an eighteen-year-old college student, intent on making my own plans for my own life. I appreciated all that the adults in my life had done for me up to that time, but I thought "growing up" meant relieving them of their responsibility and charting my own course. It was going to be my own business to choose my path, partner, and philosophy of living. I had never opened a Bible so had never read any biblical concepts on the subject.

But one day all that changed. God told Jeremiah that he had a plan for his life when Jeremiah was young and inexperienced, and he told me the same when I was young and inexperienced, too. One day I met a girl who was marching to the beat of another drummer. She told me I would never be happy until I connected with God. She had a meaningful life, a sense of purpose, and an unshakable faith in a higher being. She told me that God in love had planned for her—and that he had done the same for me. I was fascinated, not least because of her vibrant personality that I knew was somehow connected with her faith.

Compared to hers, my own life with all my plans appeared colorless and insipid. Could it be that God was a personal God who cared about me and planned for me in love? Step-by-step my new friend led me to the Cross of Christ and a Savior who died for me in order that I might live with him forever.

When I asked him to forgive my sin, my arrogant self-reliance, and my godless independence, I found myself at the beginning of a great adventure—living life according to the grand cosmic plan of God. It's a wonderful thing to find the Lord in your youth. I thank God for his grace that found me while I still had a lifetime to love and serve him.

Who is making the plans for your life? You? Your parents, teachers, or friends? Do you know that God has a wonderful plan for your life and that you will never be satisfied until you find that plan by submitting your whole self to him?

God told Jeremiah that before he even formed him in his mother's body he had already figured out the master plan for his life. "Before I formed you in the womb I knew [approved] you," he told him (Jeremiah 1:5). Think about it. Before Jeremiah existed for anyone else to know, God knew him. And before I was me to know, God knew me. He as surely has plans for you and me as he had for Jeremiah. Before we were conceived in the womb, he knew us! In fact, this knowing and purposeful choosing of God predates our conception.

Like any loving father, our heavenly Father has a plan and purpose for all of his children. In fact, the Bible says, "'I know the plans I have for you,' declares the Lord, 'plans to prosper you and not to harm you, plans to give you hope and a future'" (Jeremiah 29:11). God was talking to Israel, but he wants to give all of his children hope and a future.

GOD HAS A PLAN FOR YOU

Even after becoming a Christian, I still had difficulty grasping the "plan" idea. The reason for this was that I had a very beautiful sister. I have always adored her and never felt bad about her being the center of attention. It was no problem to me at all that the boys wanted to get to know me so they could get to know her! But even though I was more than grateful to bask in her glory, the inevitable happened, and I developed a very low self-image.

I didn't know there are no ugly sisters in God's sight. I had to learn that he is a purposeful God who had sweet reasons for making me just as I am. It's hard to understand that God likes me when I don't like myself. I found it difficult to believe that he had a special plan for *me*.

If we don't think very highly of ourselves, it's hard to believe that God planned for us as thoroughly as he planned for Jeremiah, Moses, Abraham, David, Matthew, Mark, Luke, or John. Of course, it's easy to believe God had a plan for those Bible people or for great Christian leaders such as Augustine, Billy Graham, Dwight L. Moody, or Mother Teresa! But then we say to ourselves, *I'm just plain ordinary me. Why would God think I'm special?* Or we think we are too old or too young, too black or too white, too rich or too poor, too uneducated or too disadvantaged. Well, if we feel like this, we are in good company. Jeremiah felt just like that, and he told God so.

"I am only a child," he protested, only to hear God say, "Do not say, 'I am only a child.' You must go to everyone I send you to and say whatever I command you" (Jeremiah 1:6-7). God thinks highly enough of each of us to have been thinking and planning for us for all eternity! Now if that doesn't make us feel significant, I don't know what will.

Of course, there are other reasons that we may find it difficult to consider God's plan for our lives. Perhaps our own plans are perfectly satisfying and we are so busy at work or play or even in church affairs that we don't take the time to "star gaze."

Have you ever called a child in from play because you have plans for him? Maybe you are going shopping for clothes for him, and you have planned to stop and have ice cream afterwards at a favorite place. Have you ever had to insist that your plans are more important than his plans and that he should curtail the playing and come and get ready? "You must come in now," you insist. "I have plans." You have thought the plan out, and now it is time to invite the child to participate, but he is too busy with his own activity to think that your plans are even better than his!

Who of us in this situation has not had to listen to Jeremiah-like protests, such as, "I'm too busy," or, "I'm having too much fun," or, "I don't feel like eating ice cream today." And who of us has not replied, "But you must come, and you must come now."

The calling of God has a "mustness" about it. He knows how much better his ways are than our ways. No matter how busy we are with other things or how much fun we think we are having, our heavenly Father's will for us needs to be done. His plans for us are the most important plans and are certainly the ones that will bring us the most joy.

GOD CALLS YOU TO A RELATIONSHIP WITH HIM

In his book *The Call* (Word Publishing, 1998), Os Guinness describes two types of "calls" that God has on every believer's life. The first call has to do with our salvation. The second call has to do with each person's individual vocation and tasks. We will discuss the secondary call in the next chapter. But here we will take a look at God's primary call on our lives.

The plan of God is first and foremost for you to have a relationship with him. He wants you to identify with his will and work in this world, but he wants you first to identify with him. He invites you to be forgiven and enjoy his life in you. He wants to be your Father and desires that you be his child. This relationship with God can happen only when you realize that God was reconciling the world to himself in Christ (2 Corinthians 5:19). This reconciliation can come to pass only when you realize that your sin has separated you from God. Only the death of Christ on your behalf can put that right. When you believe that God can make you right with him, when you repent of your sin and ask his forgiveness, then he grants you his Holy Spirit. At that point your relationship with him begins. Notice I didn't say that a "religion" begins.

The fact that God calls us to a relationship rather than to a religion was a pleasant surprise to me. Religion itself had a bad connotation in my thinking. I believed that religion would get in the way of my relationships. In fact, I had the idea that religion would mess up any exciting relationship I had!

I was eighteen, at college, and having a wonderful time on the outside. But I was miserable on the inside because my life revolved around my relationships. If my relationships were going well, I was going well. Most of the time, however, they weren't going well, so I was miserable. Religion didn't interest me one little bit, but relationships did.

Then I met a girl who was, appropriately, named Grace. She obviously had a relationship with someone special—I was sure of it. She had a little secret smile playing around her mouth and a twinkle in her eye that made her look as though someone was loving her to death. Actually, someone was loving her to life! She was a Christian, the first one I ever remember meeting. Imagine my chagrin when I found out that she was "religious"! Yet she didn't act, talk, or behave as I had imagined religious people do. How on earth did she have religion *and* a relationship at the same time? She set me thinking.

The next Christian I met was the girl who told me that I needed a relationship with God. I remember thinking she was just like Grace. In fact, I was sure they were relatives! Once she explained the gospel to me, I went for it with my heart and soul. This was the relationship that would make all the other relationships in my life make sense. My sin was forgiven, and I put all my earthly relationships in God's hands from that point on. Those two girls showed me what it meant to relate to the living God, who alone could fill the inner longing for someone special in my life.

God's Plan above All Other Relationships

Because your relationship with the living God is God's primary call on your life, it has to take precedence over all other relationships in your life. In Jeremiah's case this relationship with the living God affected all his major decisions about other relationships, including marriage.

God told the prophet that he must not get married. He didn't say, "I would rather you didn't get married." He said, "You must not marry" (Jeremiah 16:2). Remember, God's plan has a "mustness" about it. God had a good reason for telling Jeremiah this. He knew what was about to happen to the nation and was sparing him the agony of watching a wife and children suffer the unspeakable horrors that were about to happen (Jeremiah 16:3-4).

As with all major decisions about the relationships of life, God will guide us and tell us what he wants for us. We are free to choose to either obey or disobey the promptings of the Spirit. We are not free, however, to choose the consequences of our actions! If Jeremiah had not allowed his relationship with God to rule all his other relationships, he would have faced even more intense personal loss and suffering.

Before I became a Christian, the girl who led me to the Lord asked me whether I was willing to stay unmarried if I became a follower of Jesus. "Why would I need to stay unmarried?" I inquired, startled. "Aren't there any Christian men around?"

"Not many," was the reply. "So by the law of averages you won't find a Christian partner."

"Then I will marry an unbeliever and win him to Christ," I answered promptly.

"That's the problem, Jill," my friend replied. "The Bible says you shouldn't do that; it's not the will of God." She explained that if marriage was in the plan of God for me, it must be only with a believer (2 Corinthians 6:14).

So right at the beginning of my Christian life I realized that my relationship with God had to be more important than any other relationship in my life. And how could it be more important if I was disregarding what he had clearly stated in his Word?

A young girl once confided to me that she was dating an unbeliever. "But I'm praying about it," she added hastily.

"Save your breath," I replied. "God has already told you not to do that. In fact, it says in Psalm 66:18, 'If I had cherished sin in my heart, the Lord would not have listened.' So save your breath and be an obedient child," I advised her. The plan of God should supersede your plans for yourself where other relationships, especially marriage, are concerned.

God's Plan above Career

Because your relationship with the living God is God's primary call on your life, that call must come first, even before your career plans. It isn't a question of which vocation you should train for or how much money you can make but rather how God has gifted you and how you can find the vocation he has had in mind for you from the beginning. All too often young people head for the training that will bring them quick prosperity.

Jeremiah discovered that the plan of God for his life meant losing his landholdings. He lamented, "I have forgotten what prosperity is" (Lamentations 3:17). This in no way means that all God's children have to be materially poor! In fact, his plans include trusting some of his people with wealth and means. But we are to hold these things lightly and not tightly, remembering that "it is he who gives you the ability to produce wealth" (Deuteronomy 8:18). We are intended to be good stewards of the resources he has given us and use them for his kingdom.

When Stuart and I went into missions, my sweet parents could not really understand it. After all, Stuart was doing well in banking, and his career was taking off. My parents had bought a lovely country home in the English lake district and would visit us on the way there for weekends.

One day my mother said wistfully, "I love coming to your house, Jill. God lives here!" "Here" was a tiny cottage in our missions community.

Taking a deep breath, I answered, "Yes, Mom, and I would rather live in my cottage with Jesus than in my castle without him."

It was true! It was really true. I had known the privilege of wealth, but the privilege of serving the Lord was wealth beyond my wildest dreams. Like Jeremiah, I had "forgotten what prosperity is," but we had Jesus, and he was enough.

I realized then that there are poor little rich people, but there are also rich little poor people—and I was one of them! Our relationship with the living God had led us to lay down our secular employment in order to serve him full-time. This was the plan of God for our lives, and it was all good.

What has God gifted you to do? What has he laid on your heart? Diligently seek his plan for your life's work. You will find the greatest joy and peace when you are in the middle of his will—no matter where it takes you!

God's Plan above Personal Well-Being

Because your relationship with the living God is God's primary call on your life, you must obey whether it is good for your health or not. It is said that the missionaries who were the first to go to Africa from Europe packed their goods in coffins, knowing that in all probability they would not return from the mission field alive. It is easy to fall prey to the "health and wealth gospel" these days. But for some of us, obeying the call of God may well mean ill health because we will be living in countries where there is little medical help available. God has not called his children to flowery beds of ease but rather, as Paul instructed Timothy, to enduring "hardship . . . like a good soldier of Christ Jesus" (2 Timothy 2:3). Jeremiah lamented, "He has made my skin and my flesh grow old and has broken my bones" (Lamentations 3:4).

As Jeremiah responded to God's call to a relationship with himself and abandoned his own plans for his life, he found the reason for his existence and for living—and this despite his difficult circumstances.

It is so sad to see people living their lives without a clue as to what God wants them to be or to do. It does not need to be like this. The answer is in a relationship with God that leads you to discover his plan for your life. When you connect with that, you will find that you get what you wanted out of life after all. Have you gotten what you wanted out of life? Or are you thinking that around the corner of tomorrow the answer is waiting for you?

Some time ago a rather remarkable piece of writing came across my desk. I do not know the source, but the writer hit the nail on the head.

It was spring but it was summer I wanted.
The warm days and the grand outdoors.
It was summer but it was fall I wanted.
The colorful leaves and the cool dry air.
It was fall but it was winter I wanted.
The beautiful snow and the joy of the holiday season.
It was winter but it was spring I wanted.
The warmth and the blossoming of nature.

I was a child but it was adulthood I wanted.
The freedom and the respect.
I was 20 but it was 30 I wanted.
To be mature and sophisticated.
I was middle aged but it was 20 I wanted.
The youth and the free spirit.

I was retired but it was middle age I wanted,
The presence of mind without limitations.
My life was over,
But I never got what I wanted!

Jason Lehman, fourteen years old

Some people live all their lives and never get what they want because they are always looking in the wrong places. They feel a call to make money or explore the world. They look for happiness in material things, religion, a satisfying career, or their relationships. Somehow they know that the secret of getting what they want lies in the realm of their relationships, but if no one tells them about the one supreme relationship with God, they will get to the end of their life and say, "I never got what I wanted." How thankful I am that Janet Smith took the time and trouble to make sure I heard the glad Good News.

Someone needs to tell a searching world, "No man can ever love you enough, no child can ever need you enough, no friend can ever be friend enough, only Jesus!" What a blessing that God can make his voice heard above the cacophony of voices in the world and say, "Before I formed you in the womb I knew you. Now you need to know me! Then you will have what you really want."

Fyodor Dostoyevsky said, "The secret of man's being is not only to live, but to live for something definite." Søren Kierkegaard said, "The goal is to find the idea for which I can live and die." The problem with most people is that they have nothing definite to do and nothing definite to believe. They have never found the reason for which they can live and die. Once you come into a relationship with God through Christ, you will have a definite reason for living. To know God and what he has in mind for you is to find purpose and meaning, a reason for being.

GOD WILL BE FAITHFUL TO YOU

When we have accepted God's primary call on our lives—to a relationship with him—we know that no matter what plans of ours must change and no matter where he takes us, he will always be faithful. This gives us a sense of peace within, even if everything is not at peace around us.

For Jeremiah, nothing made sense in the political realm, the personal realm, or the prophetical realm. He lived in the last days of the nation of Judah when King Manasseh was on the throne. In his book *Jeremiah: The Prophet Who Wouldn't Quit* (Victor Books, 1984), William Peterson says, "It's hard to imagine a more horrendous monarch than [Manasseh]. His reign was bloody, vile and filthy pagan. He could go down in history books with Nero, Attila the Hun, and Adolf Hitler."

As a small boy, Jeremiah would have heard reports from the priests who lived around him in Anathoth about the goings-on in the capital city of Jerusalem. The king had sacrificed his own son on an altar, set up shrines to worship foreign deities, and allowed homosexuals to roam around the temple. There was crime in the streets and a wholesale turning away from the Jewish faith and ways.

There were military threats from the west, raids from the east, and scary reports about Egypt's Pharaoh Neco and Babylon's Nebuchadnezzar. It was not a very safe or happy place to live! Nothing seemed to make sense anymore, and no one could figure out what it all meant.

Then God let a man into his secrets. He began to explain the meaning behind the events in the world to Jeremiah in order that he might understand that things were not out of control despite all evidence to the contrary. God was the reason behind everything in the universe and all the events on earth.

Could it be that God's plans for us might include living in a country that is ruled by a man like Manasseh? *Surely he would not allow that to happen,* we think. Yet he allowed it to happen to Jeremiah. He allowed Joseph to be sold into Egypt as a slave—and by his brothers no less! He permitted Daniel to keep the lions company, and he was about to permit Nebuchadnezzar to sack Jerusalem.

Are you living in a land where political chaos reigns? Take a lesson from Jeremiah. Where you are living is the place God has cho-

sen for you to live. Accepting that brings peace and, what is more, a
sense of calling to take every opportunity to use the situation for divine ends. When "Manasseh" reigns, God's people have a great opportunity to use the situation for the spread of the gospel. In the
plan of God problems can be a platform for God.

When Communism ruled Eastern Europe, a Christian grandmother found herself in a family of Communists. She lived with her
daughter, who was the leader of the party in the area. Her daughter's
child loved her very much, and though the grandmother's heart was
breaking to see her daughter and her husband raising the child an
atheist, and though "Manasseh" reigned, she accepted the fact that
nothing can happen to a believer outside the will of God, outside his
plan. So she set about telling the small child about him.

This was no easy task. Both the government and her family had
forbidden her to tell anyone about the Lord, yet she knew God had
called her to tell everyone about him. Who better to tell her own
family than she? God had put her in this very family for this very
reason. She knew she was in the plan of God, whichever political
force happened to be in power.

So she would pull the small child up on her knee and whisper in
her little ear, "God loves you." That was all she was able to do. After
whispering this great good news, she would put her finger to her lips
and say, "Shhh."

Much later, when the grandmother was gone and the girl had
grown up, Communism fell. One day the granddaughter heard a
preacher from the West preaching the gospel openly in the market
square. Going up to him, she asked, "Can you tell me about the God
who loves me?" He did, and she came to faith.

Perhaps your reaction to such stories is to dismiss them. Perhaps
you can accept that it might be the will of God for the grandmother
to live under Communism, but it is inconceivable that *you* should.
Maybe it was the plan of God to have a "Manasseh" calling the
shots, but you can't believe it could ever be God's plan for *you* to
have such a leader!

God's will, however, takes into account who is on the throne and who is in political power. Remember that "the king's heart is in the hand of the Lord; he directs it . . . wherever he pleases" (Proverbs 21:1). This is a lesson for America. At every presidential election, my husband reminds panicked voters, "It isn't a case of who is in the great White House but rather who is on the great white throne!" Jeremiah had his politics right; his Lord reigned in the affairs of men. Perhaps Jeremiah often consoled himself with Psalm 2:

> Why do the nations conspire and the peoples plot in vain? The kings of the earth take their stand and the rulers gather together against the Lord and against his Anointed One. "Let us break their chains," they say, "and throw off their fetters." The One enthroned in heaven laughs; the Lord scoffs at them. Then he rebukes them in his anger and terrifies them in his wrath, saying, "I have installed my King on Zion, my holy hill." (vv. 1-6)

As Job said, "No plan of [God] can be thwarted" (Job 42:2), and that includes the plan he has for your life and mine and for his relationship with us, whatever the problems in our own generation.

The Bible continues with its history lesson. Manasseh died, and his son Amon took over. He was a carbon copy of his father, but someone eliminated him two years later. Amon's young son Josiah took the throne at the tender age of eight.

Have you ever wondered how a godly king like Josiah could come out of a family of Manassehs and Amons? It is a source of wonder to see a child who had no models of anything but evil around him make good! It is also a source of hope.

For years Stuart and I worked with teenagers in Western Europe. Many of them had relatives that closely resembled Manasseh and Amon. Over and over again God reached down into these situations and redeemed the children. Maybe you yourself came out of such an environment. The authority figures in our lives may intimidate us, but they don't intimidate him!

By the time little Josiah was eight years old, the people had given up hope of getting a decent king. Imagine their surprise when, in the eighth year of Josiah's reign, at the age of sixteen, he "began to seek the God of his father David" (2 Chronicles 34:3). How does an Amon produce a Josiah? He doesn't; God does! Someone was praying! Maybe it was Jeremiah!

Jeremiah doubtless heard the incredible news about a teenager his age making spiritual waves in Jerusalem. This was surely a huge encouragement to the boy, as by now many of the priests who lived in his hometown had thrown in the towel. Some were following the lead of the priests in Jerusalem by setting up shrines in Anathoth. His heart must have quickened with excitement as everyone began to talk about the reforms the young king had bravely inaugurated in the capital.

In the twelfth year of Josiah's reign he began to clean up the temple and pull down the altars that had been set up all over the land. The year was 626 B.C., and Jeremiah was around eighteen years of age, when suddenly "the word of the Lord came to" him (Jeremiah 1:4).

The words *came to* really mean "happened to." The phrase occurs in the Old Testament 123 times and suggests "self-existent power that manifests itself and is able to transform what it touches." It surely transformed Jeremiah! God's primary call of Jeremiah to a relationship with him was an experience that the prophet would revisit again and again in the hard years to come. It was this primary call that kept him keeping on when anyone else would have given up. Despite the worst that people could do to Jeremiah, he did his best for God and finished the race set before him. He just wouldn't quit!

I remember seeing a poster in a small boy's bedroom. It showed a very dispirited youngster sitting on the bench after an obviously disappointing game of football. His shoulders were drooping, and the caption at the top of the poster said it all: "I quit." At the bottom of the poster was a cross and a form upon it. The caption across the cross said succinctly, "I didn't!" The message was clear.

God called Jeremiah to himself and promised to be all that he needed. He said, "I will be faithful to you; now you be faithful to me, and I will give you faith enough to finish." For this totally daunting task, Jeremiah would need a faith that worked.

God's primary plan and call upon your life is to a relationship with him. When you are in a relationship with God—when he is the center of your life—then you can have faith in all of his plans for you.

TIME OUT

These worksheets can be used in groups, in church classes, or with individuals as a discipling tool. They can also be used in a personal quiet time.

Take Time

1. Read Jeremiah 1:1-7. Do you believe that God calls everyone, or just prophets and priests?
2. How does Jeremiah address God in the first part of verse 6? In light of this, why does Jeremiah's reply in the second part of verse 6 seem strange?
3. Do you believe that God has a plan for your life? Why or why not?
4. Which of the following words best describes your understanding of what God wants of you? Discuss.

  • Religion
  • Ritual
  • Relationship

5. When it comes to your plans for your life, which of the following is the hardest area to let God plan?

  • Other relationships (such as marriage)
  • Career
  • Personal well-being

6. Review the poem by Jason Lehman on pages 34 and 35. Share your reactions.
7. Review and discuss the political problems in Jeremiah's day. Does God mention them to the prophet in his initial call? What inference do you draw from that?
8. What struck you about the story of the grandmother living under Communism? What parallels from that religious and political situation can you draw today?
9. Read Psalm 2. Make a list of all that you learn about God,

about kings (world leaders), and about the psalmist. Share your list with the group.

Prayer Time

1. Praise God for his plan.
2. Pray for the leaders of the earth and their children. Who knows but that your prayers may help to bring about the appearance of another "Josiah."
3. Pray for the church and its leaders.
4. Pray for godly fathers and mothers who are living in hostile environments and are trying to bring up their children to know and love the Lord.
5. Pray for yourself and the application of this lesson to your life.

A Letter to God

Write a letter to God responding to his word to your heart.

CHAPTER FOUR
FAITH IN GOD'S CALL

————— ✿ —————

HIS WORK IN YOUR HAND

Before you were born I set you apart;
I appointed you as a prophet to the nations.
JEREMIAH 1:5

"HOW DO I 'BE' THE CHRISTIAN I'VE BECOME?" I ASKED THE girl who had just led me to Christ.

"That's really bad English, Jill," she replied with a laugh. "But I know what you mean. Becoming a Christian is one thing; being the Christian you've become is another."

I found out that being a Christian was a whole lot harder than becoming one. It's a bit like being born. I can't remember my birth. I do, however, remember lots about my development.

Having many grandchildren to observe has reminded me about those periods of growth and development, and one of those stages is a sheer delight to watch. It is the stage where children who have been born begin to know it. They become aware of their 'being,' of who they are and what they are. It usually coincides with their first words. So Drew, our eighteen-month-old grandson, would spend his happy days rushing around life saying things like "I be hot" or "I be cold" or "I be naked" or "I be hungry." One day I was there to hear him come to the momentous discovery "I be me!"

Part of that discovery is the next realization that "I be me" for a purpose. Why am I who I am? Every human being wonders about this at some stage. I am who I am, of course, in order to relate to who God is. The God who gave me my "am-ness" wants me to understand what my "am-ness" is for. God made Jeremiah aware that he made

43

him for himself and he had work for him to do. God wants to make you aware of the very same thing.

In the last chapter we explored the first, or primary, call of God on our lives—which is to a relationship with him. In this chapter we will discover that God also has a secondary call on our lives. As Os Guinness has noted in his book *The Call*, this secondary call is to tasks or vocations—the work God has appointed us to do. This includes both career plans and the minor daily tasks that come as part of everyday life. We can experience a sense of calling every day as God sets our agendas. Part of God's plan for all his people is to put his work in our hands, and part of being spiritually mature is this sense of calling to this work.

God doesn't leave us guessing what our job is, either. When he called Jeremiah, he had very specific instructions for him that included what he wanted Jeremiah to do, where he wanted him to do it, and what the results would be. God also gave Jeremiah a small glimpse into the big picture.

In two parables God explained to his servant that "disaster will be poured out on all who live in the land" (Jeremiah 1:14). This judgment was just and right because Israel had played the fool and deserved God's wrath. "I will pronounce my judgments on my people because of their wickedness in forsaking me" (Jeremiah 1:16). Jeremiah was convinced of God's perfect right to do as he willed with his own, and he had no doubt as to the truth that he needed to convey.

But when God called Jeremiah to convey the truth about the situation to Israel, Jeremiah was totally overwhelmed by the task. He was able to appreciate that God was calling him to a relationship with him, but he balked at the call to this specific task. He was sure that God had called the wrong man for the job. "'Ah, Sovereign Lord,' I said, 'I do not know how to speak; I am only a child'" (Jeremiah 1:6). The Lord, however, confirmed his confidence in Jeremiah.

YOU ARE APPOINTED TO YOUR TASKS

God told Jeremiah, "Before you were born I set you apart [consecrated you for my special use]; I appointed you as a prophet to the nations" (Jeremiah1:5). God commissioned, appointed, or ordained Jeremiah as his spokesman before the foundation of the world. And one day Jeremiah became aware of his divine appointment.

Are you aware of your divine appointment? Are you convinced about God's truth concerning his lost world and what he wants you to do about it? Your appointment and my appointment will be different from Jeremiah's appointment, but all will be just as important as others in the bigger scheme of things.

Again, in his book *The Call*, Os Guinness says,

> *Our primary calling as followers of Christ is by him, to him, and for him.* First and foremost we are called to Someone (God), not to something (such as motherhood, politics, or teaching) or to somewhere (such as the inner city or Outer Mongolia).
>
> *Our secondary calling, considering who God is as sovereign, is that everyone, everywhere, and in everything should think, speak, live, and act entirely for him.* We can therefore properly say as a matter of secondary calling that we are called to homemaking or to the practice of law or to art history. But these and other things are always the secondary, never the primary calling. They are "callings" rather than the "calling." They are our personal answer to God's address, our response to God's summons. Secondary callings matter, but only because the primary calling matters most.

As Jeremiah was to discover, when he was up to his neck in the slime pit because of his secondary calling (his task), it was his primary calling (his relationship with God) that kept him faithful and sane.

Finding Joy in the Doing

So often we can get thoroughly fed up with the callings, or tasks, that we do for God in Christian service. If we don't have our primary calling overruling and overshadowing our secondary callings, we quit or at least lose all joy in the journey. We also need to sense the huge importance of our secondary callings. These callings have been as much in the mind of God for us as was our primary calling. Knowing this changes our attitude toward everything we do.

You need to ask yourself, *What is driving my ministry activity?* Are you running the church nursery because someone at church asked you to or because you believe that God (who is calling the shots) nudged that person to ask you to? Are you convinced that this activity you are engaged in is the reason God made you in the first place?

A cartoon in a Christian magazine showed an old lady sitting in the church nursery in a rocking chair. She had been there a long time. The caption underneath the picture said, "I only came in here 30 years ago because Hilda wanted to go to the bathroom!" You can laugh at this, unless *you* are the one who has been stuck in that same rocking chair and are not sure you should have been there.

If you find yourself in a similar dilemma, let me ask you this: What has kept you at your post? If God has kept you there because you discerned that this was one of your secondary callings, then you will be confident, happy, and satisfied to be there. If, on the other hand, you are there because Hilda asked you to be there or because no one else would take a turn, or just out of sheer habit, you will have no joy in the doing. You run the risk of looking back and asking yourself, *What could I have done with all those hours spent in that rocking chair?*

A missionary in the Caribbean once told me, "I have served at this post for thirty-six years. I have been a missionary wife and full-time pastor's wife all this time. If I have one regret, it is that I have been in the pew every time the church door was open. I have not missed one wedding or funeral. Looking back, I question why. I think of many, many times I did not need to be there. I realize that I could have accomplished so much if I had allowed God to tell me where he wanted me and what he wanted me to do and not let others' expectations drive my actions."

How do you know if you are truly *in* God's secondary calling on your life? Listen to God's still small voice. He will tell you. And then, with some strange internal knowledge, you'll say, *Yes, this is the particular secondary calling he had in mind for me before he made me.*

Letting God Set Your Agenda

These secondary callings can be practical callings or spiritual callings. In fact, all practical callings of God are really spiritual! But we tend to imagine that doing something practical is somehow less significant.

I remember one of our married children needing help. Our son called me one day and asked, "Mom, could you possibly come and stay with the kids? We need to get away." The young couple was trying to sort out some problems in their marriage, and this was an emergency. I responded at once with, "Of course, I'll be there, and I'll be there tomorrow." Then I asked the Lord what I was going to do about the meetings I had scheduled the next day and the next week. This crisis had not been on my agenda!

"It was on *mine!*" God responded. After talking it over with God, my husband and I discerned that this was the thing that God had always had in mind for the next ten days of my life. It was a secondary calling.

Not that it was an easy calling, but my heart had been invested with a divine necessity to be there. There were four children under five years of age to care for! I found it wonderful but challenging. One night I was so exhausted that I said, "Good night, kids." Then I went to bed and left them all up! Yet in all the tiredness, I was aware every day that there was only one place on earth I was meant to be at that particular moment in my timeline on earth, and that was right there with that little family. My appointed heart told me so.

Five weeks later I was back home standing in front of hundreds of women teaching a Bible study. Exactly the same assurance filled my heart. This was precisely the place God wanted me to be. My appointed heart was quite definite about that also.

Because God wanted me doing those things—one practical and one spiritual—both were spiritual actions. I was fulfilling the central purpose of my life in both cases. I was being the me I was meant to be! Called to put God first in my decisions, these activities were what he had told me were "first today." This is exciting! It means that the most menial tasks are invested with a divine importance that helps us see the task through. It reminds me of a plaque that my mother-in-law had over her kitchen sink: "Divine service conducted three times daily here!"

Consider the callings of Jeremiah and his scribe, Baruch. Jeremiah received the word of the Lord. What an extraordinary spiritual experience that must have been. Baruch put those words on a scroll by hand—twenty years' worth of them. One task was not more "spiritual" than the other, for both tasks had been commissioned by God.

Baruch belonged to a noble family and was a man of great achievements. He was certainly a respected scribe in Israel. He was the writer and accomplished the practical side of the ministry with Jeremiah. This did not mean that the practical things Baruch did were not spiritual. If only we could catch the spiritual worth of all practical ministries, we would have a great sense of achievement and satisfaction.

God set Jeremiah and Baruch aside, or consecrated them, for the tasks he had for them to do. If only we believed that God has set us aside as surely as he set these two men aside, our mothering, our business life, or our social activities would look altogether different.

Perhaps you need to stop reading this book and sit quietly before the Lord. Reaffirm your first call, which is to a relationship with him. Then ask him to make you sure of your secondary callings—the jobs he has for you to do as an outflow of this relationship. Life could be very different for you from this moment on! The next step after having this conversation with God is to realize that your "appointed heart" is also your "anointed heart."

YOU ARE ANOINTED TO PERFORM

God has appointed you to a task that he has anointed you to perform. God never calls without equipping! Someone has said, "God doesn't call the equipped, he equips the called." As far as I can see, "anointing" means that as you are in the midst of a duty, somewhere in the depths of your being comes a great shout of "God confidence"—an "I can do this" sound. "This is possible," you realize, where before it looked impossible. In fact, God is a God of the possible, and being anointed means living in the good of the possibilities of God! We receive this anointing from the Holy Spirit.

Consecrated by the Spirit

In the Bible, anointing oil symbolized the presence of the Lord's Spirit to give a person wholeness. The word for anointing that is used in the Old Testament means to "consecrate to service." God anointed prophets, priests, and kings and set them apart for service. For that matter, pots and pans were anointed and set apart too! Anything or anyone called to be used for temple service was set apart by anointing. I may be a priest or a pan—one is as consecrated as the other!

In the Old Testament only certain persons and objects were anointed for office, but in the New Testament all believers receive the anointing by the Holy Spirit. First John 2:20 says, "You have an anointing from the Holy One, and all of you know the truth." He later adds, "The anointing you received from him remains in you, and you do not need anyone to teach you. But as his anointing teaches you about all things and as that anointing is real, not counterfeit—just as it has taught you, remain in him" (v. 27). This was predicted by Jeremiah, who talked about the promised New Covenant era:

> "This is the covenant I will make with the house of Israel
> after that time," declares the Lord. "I will put my law in
> their minds and write it on their hearts. I will be their God,
> and they will be my people. No longer will a man teach his
> neighbor, or a man his brother, saying, 'Know the Lord,'
> because they will all know me, from the least of them to the
> greatest," declares the Lord. (Jeremiah 31:33-34)

So when the Holy Spirit comes into a believer's life, he comes to teach, guide, and empower. He teaches and guides us to the truth, saves us from error, and gives us strength to hold on to that truth. Jesus said that the Holy Spirit would guide his people into all truth.

He can help you read the Bible and interpret it as you are reading. He will help you understand and interpret it correctly.

When I first became a Christian, I had never read the Bible for myself. I was at college in Cambridge among students who were investigating all the religious philosophies under the sun. I didn't know if an apostle was the wife of an epistle! How would I know how to interpret the Bible?

I prayed one day, "Lord, please deliver me from error." I didn't know that John had prayed for that for the readers of his epistle. He was writing to people who couldn't read or write, as well as to the educated. They, too, lived among other philosophies. He said, "You have an anointing from the Holy One, and all of you know the truth." So as God promised, he makes it possible for you to know the truth and to discern error. And he consecrates you, sets you apart, to serve him.

Empowered by the Spirit

We hear much today about empowering. Whole industries have sprung up to empower people in all areas of their lives. The Holy Spirit will empower us to do the tasks that we have no power to do alone. He comes to help those who are helpless. He comes to strengthen and inspire. In other words, he is in your life in order to anoint you for your appointed task—the task he assigned to you before you were you to know!

For me this empowering often comes when I need words that work—words that convince, convict, or convert the people to whom I am talking. Words are necessary in the calling he has given me, and I have experienced this empowering by the Holy Spirit over and over again. It is as if words that struggle to get off the ground take flight and arrive at their destination. It is perfectly all right for me to bank on him doing this for me. In fact, it has been the habit of my life to ask him to give wings to my words. Whether I am struggling to find a word of encouragement for a single parent, a word of comfort for a bereaved husband, or words for a talk for students, women, a congregation, or a conference, I pray with confidence:

Give my words wings, Lord.
May they alight gently on the branches of men's minds,
Bending them to the winds of your will.
May they fly high enough to touch the lofty,
Low enough to bring the breath of sweet encouragement
*   upon the downcast soul.*

Give my words wings, Lord.
May they fly swift and far,
Winning the race with the words of the worldly wise,
To the hearts of men.

Give my words wings, Lord.
See them now,
Nesting—
Down at thy feet.
Silenced into ecstasy,
Home at last.

God's work in your hands cannot be done without the anointing of the Holy Spirit. But you can bank on him to do it. If you have the Holy Spirit, you have the anointing. Remember what 1 John 2:20 says: "You have an anointing from the Holy One." Just make sure there is no known sin in your life. Trust in his promise that you have the anointing—and then go for it!

God *appoints* you to a task that he *anoints* you to perform. Then he *assists* you with the special tools that you will need.

YOU ARE ASSISTED WITH SPECIAL TOOLS

During the Second World War, Winston Churchill appealed to the allies, "Give us the tools, and we'll finish the job." You can't fight a war without weapons, and in the spiritual realm some of the weapons of warfare are gifts of the Spirit. These gifts are natural or spiritual abilities consecrated to God, tools God gives to accomplish the tasks he has in mind for you.

In the building of the temple God chose a man called Bezalel of

the tribe of Judah and "filled him with the Spirit of God, with skill
. . . in all kinds of crafts—to make artistic designs for work in gold,
silver and bronze, to cut and set stones, to work in wood, and to engage in all kinds of craftsmanship" (Exodus 31:2-5). Then God appointed and anointed another man, Oholiab, to teach others. And
God filled many people "with skill to do all kinds of work as crafts-
men, designers, embroiderers in blue, purple and scarlet yarn and
fine linen, and weavers" (Exodus 35:35). And God gave them this
instruction: "So Bezalel, Oholiab and every skilled person to whom
the Lord has given skill and ability to know how to carry out all the
work of constructing the sanctuary are to do the work just as the
Lord has commanded" (Exodus 36:1). Notice that the Spirit enabled these men and those they taught to finish the tasks that God
had called them to accomplish.

After a meeting I sat next to a young woman who looked very
downcast. "What's the matter?" I inquired.

"I feel so useless," she replied. "I can't do anything spiritual, like
teach or preach. All I can do is make things, like crafts."

I showed her the verses from Exodus and then told her, "Jesus
was a carpenter for thirty years and a preacher for three." Her face
lit up. "Do you think those thirty years were wasted—that he was
on hold?" I asked her. "He could have said, 'I feel useless, all I can
do is make things!' Those thirty years in Nazareth and the tasks he
accomplished that appeared to be so obscure were ordained of God
just as much as his three years on the road."

The important thing is to find what God has gifted you to do.
He will give you all the necessary skills to finish the tasks he has
given you. They may be gifts that don't "look" as spiritual as other
gifts, but if they are God's gifts given you for God's time in God's
place, you can bank on the filling of his Spirit to exercise them. In
other words, his anointing, his blessing, his understanding are as
necessary for the practical callings as for the so-called spiritual ones.

His plan in your life means his work in your hands, and you can
be sure it is work he has chosen and gifted you to do. God left Jere-

miah no doubt as to the nature of the work he had put in Jeremiah's hands. This was all part of the plan of God for his life.

After God had called Jeremiah to himself and to his work, he encouraged him by promising that his strength would be made perfect in Jeremiah's weakness. God would give him words to say when he felt like a child. He would make him bold when his knees were knocking. God told Jeremiah not to be afraid but to trust. But God also gave him special tools to do the job.

Special Clothing

"Get yourself ready!" God said to Jeremiah. "Stand up and say to them whatever I command you. Do not be terrified by them, or I will terrify you before them" (Jeremiah 1:17).

The King James Version of the Bible begins this verse with the words "Gird up thy loins," a phrase that means to tie up a long flowing robe in order to run without encumbrance. Another way of putting it is "Get up and get dressed" (NLT). God was saying, "Dress yourself with clothes I have prepared for you so you can run freely to do my will."

I have been impressed with the way modern parents encourage their young children to choose which clothes to wear each day. As early as four or five, young children think about the activities of the day and learn which clothes are appropriate for which activity. The parents give them freedom to choose.

God gives us that freedom, too. We need to dress ourselves suitably for the work of the Lord. We need to choose "clothing" that will not hinder us in getting the job done. There is a tough job ahead for God's soldiers, and we need to learn to dress our souls appropriately for the battle.

God warned Jeremiah that he would have many enemies. Being forewarned was being forearmed. God would make him a tower of strength and help him to overcome all his inadequacies. He was not to lose his nerve. In fact, God knew better than Jeremiah did that Jeremiah could fulfill his calling because God had made him ideal for the job. Knowing in advance what he would ask him to do, God had made him able to do it.

God believed in Jeremiah; God knew he could do it. To have someone believe in you is all the empowering it takes for you to move mountains. To have God believe you can do it should be all you need to face the foe. To know I am part of the plan, to be empowered by the Spirit, and to be assured of his presence can help me get up, get dressed, go out, and tell the world whatever God tells me to say.

Jeremiah would need special clothing because his ministry would be both destructive and constructive. The emphasis was, however, to be on the destructive side. "See, today I appoint you over nations and kingdoms to uproot and tear down, to destroy and overthrow, to build and to plant" (Jeremiah 1:10). God also told Jeremiah that those who heard his message would not appreciate it.

Many of us have the idea that God would not call us to a difficult task—only to a glorious one. I would prefer to "build up and plant" in people's lives rather than "tear down and destroy." I would hope he would fill my mouth with comforting words, not confronting words. But sometimes we are given unpleasant messages to deliver, and that takes extra grace and enabling. The battle often begins when we must point out sin or tell someone an unpalatable truth.

I hate it when I have to be tough with someone. I would much rather be tender. Often it is only when I realize that it is a matter of obedience to the Lord that I comply. Basically, it is sheer selfishness that causes me to back off from a confronting ministry. I want the person to like me, and I don't want to hurt our relationship.

Parents face this dilemma. Perhaps a teenager needs rebuking. But you know this will cause a battle royal, and you hate that. *What will happen to my relationship with my child if I bring up this particular issue?* we worry. But someone has to take a risk when it is necessary to say the right thing, and who better than a parent? Sometimes it is time to "uproot and tear down, to destroy and overthrow"!

Maybe your child will not like you very much for a while, but if you obey the promptings of the Spirit and deliver the truth in love,

God will look after the results. You will have the satisfaction of knowing you were appointed and anointed as his messenger on this occasion, and then assisted with the power to do it.

Talking to a Christian teenager, I struggled to address a topic that I knew would jeopardize our relationship. She was dating a boy who was antagonistic to the faith, and I could see that this was affecting her own beliefs more than she was willing to admit.

Venturing to offer some unasked-for advice, I began to discuss the situation. "I'm praying about it," she assured me, bristling.

I was tempted to back off. After all, it was none of my business. But I knew it *was* my business. I was a youth leader, and I knew this was one of my secondary callings. What was more, the girl was in my Bible study group, and I had led her to Christ. I knew the message God was telling me to give her, but it was a message of destruction, and I didn't want to deliver it. In the end she assured me again that she was praying about it and asking God to show her if this was the man for her. I finally said, "Don't waste your breath. God will not listen to your prayers because he has already told you he doesn't want you to be tied up with an unbeliever." I showed her 2 Corinthians 6:14. She read it and then angrily ran out of the room.

It is hard to be obedient to your appointed task, isn't it? Jeremiah was to experience unbelievable reactions to his unsought words of spiritual advice, but he faithfully stuck with his tough assignments to the end.

Twice God tells Jeremiah, "I am with you and will rescue you" (Jeremiah 1:8, 19). As you read this man's story, you may be tempted to wonder about that. Did anyone ever accept his hard sayings? Didn't the prophet get hunted like an animal and tortured nearly to death? Yes, he did. God doesn't promise to always save you *externally*, but he always promises to save you *internally*—to give you faith for fear, peace in your problems, serenity in the storm, and faith enough to finish. He will never leave you nor forsake you, no matter how difficult the task. He who has appointed and anointed will assist you with the power to finish.

Special Courage

What do you do when you are paralyzed with fear, when the spirit is willing but the flesh is weak? Jeremiah 1:17 continues with God's words to him: "Do not be terrified." Another translation renders it, "Don't lose your nerve." Apparently faith in God can reduce our fear to a manageable size. God tells Jeremiah he is not to allow fear to stop him from being obedient to his calling.

So what do we do if we can't chase our fears out of our hearts? Then do the task frightened! Courage is not doing God's work without any fear or apprehension. Courage is doing God's work even when you are afraid.

I learned this lesson when I was very frightened to go into an area of the world where we were in danger of being kidnapped. I knew this particular assignment was something God wanted us to do, but I was so frightened I couldn't commit myself to it. I read a little quote in a book that said, "Courage is fear that has said its prayers." So I said my prayers. I told God that I was very fearful but that I would not allow myself to be terrified into staying home. I would go whether he took the fear away or not. Courage is doing without the courage.

God told Jeremiah, "Today I have made you a fortified city, an iron pillar and a bronze wall to stand against the whole land. . . . They will fight against you but will not overcome you, for I am with you and will rescue you" (Jeremiah 1:18-19). My fears never fully disappeared during that difficult and dangerous situation, but I found that God garrisoned my frightened heart and made it like a "fortified city," and I was able to do my work despite the threats of the "people of the land."

YOU ARE GOD'S ARTWORK

It is said that Michelangelo "saw" *David* in his mind's eye before he ever started crafting that uncut piece of marble. Before Michelangelo ever lifted a hammer and chisel and started to work, *David* was finished and complete. Michelangelo knew exactly what he wanted him to be. So it is with us. In God's mind we were finished before we were started, and God knows in advance what he wants us to be.

God wants to chisel the "David" out of us! So he takes the hammer of circumstances and the chisel of ministry, and he begins to chip, chip, chip away at this piece of uncut marble that is us. He uses tools of all kinds: political situations, the church, opposition, frightening circumstances, our tasks and callings. He will use anything he has to use to craft the likeness of God in us. The Master Artist has a plan. He has a definite pattern in mind as he works away on the image that will become a reality. And he never leaves his work of art until it is finished.

So next time you hear (or feel!) that *chip, chip, chipping* in your soul, take comfort that God will stick with you until the end. One day his work in you will be finished, and you will be like him!

I know I am more like Jesus because of how God has used the circumstances of life to shape me—circumstances I do not believe are by chance or merely coincidental. There was the chisel of the Second World War and of being brought up in wartime Britain. There was the chisel of college and my teacher training. Add to that the chisel of sickness and hardship. The chisel of marriage and children crafted some of the "David" out of me. Undoubtedly the chisel of disappointment and loss, of shattered dreams and broken promises played its part.

Then there is the chisel of ministry itself. The gifts and abilities God gave me have made their mark, as well as all the things that have happened to me and through me as I have exercised those gifts over forty years of Christian service. Secondary tasks and callings have changed me over the years. Teaching in the Liverpool school district brought me into close contact with a class of kids I had never met up until then. Coming from a good middle-class home, I had been unaware how the rest of the world lived. As the children of a poor district walked into my life, I became overwhelmed with the privileges I had taken so much for granted. I felt guilty that I had so much and they had so little, until I remembered that God had chosen my parents! And this choosing was for a reason. I was to use my privileges as opportunities to serve. So I got to work teaching and investing myself in the lives of these young Liverpool kids, and the shaping of my character began.

I set out to be the best teacher I could be. I learned listening skills, communication skills, and preparation skills. All these would transfer into ministry skills later on in my life. How I conducted myself as a young teacher, however, was all part of the forming of the person God had called me and equipped me to be, and it made its mark on my life.

But it has been in the circumstances that ministry has arranged that I have been the most conscious of the Master Sculptor. It has been in the areas of my dashed hopes and dreams that I have been most aware of his work in me.

For example, there was the time in our youth work when we no longer had the income to which we'd become accustomed. Oddly enough, I had not given too much thought to the financial aspect of our decision to leave the banking world and go into Christian ministry. It didn't seem very spiritual to talk about wages or remuneration in the same breath as the Lord's work.

"Where will we live?" I asked Stuart after we accepted the invitation to join the staff of Capernwray Missionary Fellowship.

"At one of the lodges on the estate," my husband replied. That was all I asked, and we duly packed up and set off for "Middle Lodge."

When we arrived at the youth center, we found that Middle Lodge was a charming gatehouse over a hundred years old. It was picturesque but a little lacking in space. It was also quite a surprise to discover another staff member also living there and showing no signs of moving out when we moved in! We didn't want to complain to anyone, so we all lived together in the tiny lodge for a while. This was one of the circumstances that ministry arranged.

The resulting situations that arose, as our companion invited all his friends to visit him whenever he chose, introduced us to a side of ministry no one had told us about. Privacy flies out the window, and nothing is "yours" when you live in community. I found this a little

alarming, to say the least. Our goods seemed to be at everyone's disposal, as were our home and our time. I began thinking all sorts of
ungodly thoughts—thoughts that I had no idea I was capable of en-
tertaining! *Chip, chip, chip* went the chisel as God began to chip away
at some of my more material and idealistic dreams.

Ministry arranges all sorts of surprises along the way. Some are
pleasant, and some are not. I learned to be available to people
twenty-four hours a day, to put our lives and our "everythings" at
God's disposal. After all, what did we have that he had not given us
in the first place? I remember the day I said to the Lord, "I realize,
dear Lord, that now that I am in ministry, I cannot have hours like
the post office! This is your home, and you are free to invite any of
your friends you wish into it." God took me at my word, and I
found out that he had some really strange friends—friends I would
never have thought to invite into our home if it had been left up to
me! However, it was some of these very friends of Jesus that have
added richly to our lives and the lives of our children over the years.

God's surprises come in many different ways. Circumstances
arise that take us off our feet. I could never have imagined myself
being alone so much, for example. My husband had joined the mission as treasurer, not as a traveling speaker. But traveling speaker
was the role that God had in mind for Stuart. This was one of those
secondary callings he had chosen for my husband before the foundation of the world. For months on end my husband traveled and
preached. My dreams of an ideal close-knit family experience disappeared. I found myself trying to explain the yawning "Daddy space"
that had appeared, and had not been on my agenda, to my children.
Seldom have I heard the "chip of the chisel" more clearly than in
those days! My selfish outer shell, which was very thick and very
hard, was being chipped away. I learned not to meddle with the plan
of God for my husband's life.

What have been some of the chisels and hammers in your life experience? Perhaps you could spend time with the Lord thinking
back to the surprises in your life. Maybe right now you are struggling with some broken dreams. Whom God chooses, he calls, and

whom he calls, he chisels. Know that God trusts you with his challenges. It's a compliment to have the Master Sculptor's full attention.

As I have learned to recognize the tools of my heavenly Michelangelo, the Master Sculptor, I have learned how deeply he loves me. I am only a work in process, and the callings or tasks along the way are simply a part of his loving eternal plan in my life.

As God "chisels the David" out of you, learn to treat all hammer blows as divine compliments. He has a work of art in mind. Faith that is able to trust him with the hammer and chisel is faith enough to finish.

> *Chiseled by the circumstances ministry arranges*
> *Hammered by the things allowed that made such drastic changes*
> *In my life and fondest dreams I'd hoped to realize,*
> *Chiseled by my circumstance—I'm chiseled down to size!*

TIME OUT
These worksheets can be used in groups, in church classes, or with individuals as a discipling tool. They can also be used in a personal quiet time.

Take Time
1. Read Jeremiah 1:1-11. Make a list of all the specific things God said to Jeremiah about the tasks he had in mind for him. What strikes you about the details of the plan? Apply this to your own life.
2. Read the Os Guinness quote on page 45. Discuss the sentence "Secondary callings matter, but only because the primary calling matters most." Do you agree?
3. Do you relate to the lady left in the nursery? Why?
4. Review Exodus 35:30–36:2. Discuss the difference between spiritual and practical gifts.
5. Read Jeremiah 1:17-19. What commands are in these verses? What promises? What warnings?
6. If you were Jeremiah, which verse would have helped you the most? frightened you most? challenged you most?
7. Read Ephesians 6:10-18. Discuss what it means to dress yourself for battle.
8. What are the chisels of happenstance and the hammers of circumstance for?

Prayer Time
1. Praise God for all the things this passage teaches you about his plan for your life.
2. Praise him for his promise in Jeremiah 1:19: "'They will fight against you but will not overcome you, for I am with you and will rescue you,' declares the Lord."
3. Pray that the secondary callings in the lives of God's people will be made clear.
4. Pray that all the people like the lady left in the nursery will find their task and place in the church.

5. What is one way you can "dress yourself for action"? Pray about it.
6. Thank God for the chisels and hammers in your life.

A Letter to God
Write a letter to God about your secondary callings and the work he has put in your hands. Or write a note about a chisel you have only just recognized.

CHAPTER FIVE

FAITH IN GOD'S WORD

HIS WORD IN YOUR MOUTH

Then the Lord reached out his hand and touched
my mouth and said to me, "Now, I have put my words
in your mouth."
JEREMIAH 1:9

DID YOU EVER WISH YOU HAD "THE GIFT OF GAB"? ARE YOU
lost for wise words to heal a hurt or right a wrong? Do you wish that
you knew just what to say to convince someone who doesn't know
the Lord to love him like you do? Have you ever longed to find a
strong enough argument that would stop someone influencing your
child to do wrong? Would you give anything to be able to easily
comfort the grieving or fearful?

"Sticks and stones may break my bones, but words will never
hurt me," asserts a children's rhyme. Wrong! Sometimes words can
hurt far more than broken bones.

When I see what is going on in society, I long to shout loud
enough to be heard. And when I feel frustrated with my own inability
to argue effectively for Christ and his kingdom, I have learned to lean
on God for encouragement and some word that will truly make a difference. I apply Scripture to myself, returning to God's words to Jeremiah. For example, "Let the one who has my word speak it faithfully"
(Jeremiah 23:28). God told Jeremiah that a true spokesman for God
is required to be faithful, not necessarily successful. Our job is to pass
on the truth of his Word, not ours, persistently, day by daily day.

Do you ever feel lost for words? You don't need to if you are a
child of God. But it is encouraging to know that even some of the
prophets felt as we do.

"HERE AM I; SEND AARON"

When God called Moses to lead the children of Israel out of Egypt and into the Promised Land, he answered, "O Lord, I have never been eloquent, neither in the past nor since you have spoken to your servant. I am slow of speech and tongue." To which the Lord replied, "Who gave man his mouth? Who makes him deaf or mute? Who gives him sight or makes him blind? Is it not I, the Lord? Now go; I will help you speak and will teach you what to say." Moses was not convinced and replied, "O Lord, please send someone else to do it" (Exodus 4:10-13). In other words, Moses' response to the call of God was, "Here am I; send Aaron!"

Have you ever felt as Moses did, that you are not good with words? Or like Jeremiah, that you are too young? I have. I was twenty-one when I began to work with teenagers. Not only was I young, I was a new believer. As opportunities began to open up, I found myself teaching adults also. Sometimes an older person would challenge me, not about what I was teaching, but about my age. Feeling insecure, I asked the Lord if I should back off. As I searched Scripture, I came across Paul's advice to young Timothy: "Don't let anyone look down on you because you are young, but set an example for the believers in speech, in life, in love, in faith and in purity" (1 Timothy 4:12).

Jeremiah felt some misgivings about his age and lack of experience, too. "I do not know how to speak; I am only a child." The Lord replied, "Do not say, 'I am only a child.' You must go to everyone I send you to and say whatever I command you" (Jeremiah 1:6-7). Apparently, spiritual gifts are for people of any age.

If only God would do it on his own, we think. Why does he use people and not angels? It seems really risky to me to trust a teenager with conveying the Word of God to the world. I have found myself pleading with God to speak as he spoke in the old days and shake my society into God-consciousness. Then I have clearly heard his voice from Scripture saying, "I have put my words in your mouth" (Jeremiah 1:9). I have had to learn all over again that God has a way of making his views and feelings known, and that is not by leaning out of heaven and hollering at us. His plan is to put *his* words in *our* mouths! His method is to tell *us,* so we can tell *others.*

There is an imaginative story that says that after Jesus went back to heaven, the angels gathered around to ask him how he had left things on earth. "Things are in good shape," he replied. "I have left my work in the hands of twelve men."

"Only twelve?" the angels asked, considerably surprised.

"Yes," Jesus answered.

"What happens if they fail?" inquired the angels.

"I have no other plans," said Jesus.

That's scary. His work is in our hands, and his Word is in our mouths. And the good news is that he asks us to pass it on even when we don't necessarily have the gift of the gab. He asks us to speak on his behalf, and the power of his Spirit working with us and through us will take care of our inadequacies.

Think of the shepherds in Bethlehem. God sent his angels and told them about Jesus. They ran to Bethlehem to see if the angels' message was true. When they found everything "just as they had been told," they went everywhere spreading "the word concerning what had been told them about this child" (Luke 2:20, 17). Do you think that these men were eloquent preachers? Do you think they were too young or too old? What training had they had? They were simply obedient, and God spoke his words through them.

One of the problems we have with speaking the truth of God is the notion that we always have to win the argument. We live in a country where sports dominate society, where winning counts and sometimes determines the value of the person playing the game. Jeremiah didn't win the game, at least in the eyes of his contemporaries, but he won it in the eyes of the Lord. Jeremiah felt incredibly inadequate to speak faithfully in his situation, but he did it anyway, despite his misgivings.

Speaking the Word faithfully doesn't mean the message is negative and destructive all the time. God told Jeremiah that he had appointed him "to uproot and tear down, to destroy and overthrow," but he had also appointed him "to build and to plant" (Jeremiah

1:10). His message was to be balanced, even though the majority of messages God gave him were on the dark side. Even so, Jeremiah was to speak justice and mercy together. And though there would be a whole lot more uprooting and tearing down going on than building and planting, the words of grace and mercy weave themselves in and out of the text of Jeremiah along with the words of wrath and judgment.

Words are weapons for good or evil, and Jeremiah was assured that he would be supplied with all the weaponry he would need to speak faithfully for God. Like a lawyer speaking on behalf of his client, Jeremiah constantly affirmed that he was speaking for God. He insisted that the messages he had for people were not his own. He said loudly and unequivocally that God had given him words to say and had appointed him to say them.

One of the problems he faced was violent opposition from the leaders of Israel. Jeremiah was a young unknown man from Anathoth, yet God kept giving him messages that were not very complimentary for the political and religious leaders of the day—men who were very much older and supposedly wiser than he. He was instructed to speak to old and young alike, to king and to commoner. He was to deliver God's word to priest and prophet. This was no easy assignment. Commoners were one thing; kings, priests, and prophets were another, especially when the building and planting messages seemed to be for the commoners while the uprooting and tearing down words were for the leaders of the nation!

When he shrank back from the prospect, God told him, "You must go to everyone I send you to and say whatever I command you. Do not be afraid of them, for I am with you and will rescue you" (Jeremiah 1:7-8). It must have been very tempting for Jeremiah to mix up his messages to be more "seeker sensitive"! Listen to one of the messages that God gave him to give to the religious leaders: "The shepherds of my people have lost their senses. They no longer follow the Lord or ask what he wants of them. Therefore, they fail completely, and their flocks are scattered" (Jeremiah 10:21, NLT).

The Lord warned the people, through Jeremiah, that he would

send down disasters on the leaders of his people, for they had destroyed and scattered the very ones they were expected to protect.

It must have been very hard to pass along all of *that* in church when the people in question were sitting in the front pew! I know the feeling. Not that I have ever had the job of passing on such messages to leaders, but I have had reason to be intimidated into compromising the gospel to authorities in another context.

"Okay, Lord, I'll Go"

It was the wild sixties in Great Britain, and I sat in a police cell talking to a tough young kid whom I had grown to love. "I can't believe I did it," he said.

"Neither can I," I replied.

"I'm done for now, aren't I?" he said, looking at me desperately.

"Actions have consequences," I replied.

"Has God finished with me?"

"His mercies never fail," I answered.

"What does that mean?"

"Nobody's too big a sinner to be forgiven. It says in the Bible that God saves to the uttermost."

"From the gutter-most to the uttermost, eh?"

"Yes."

"*I* am."

"You am what?"

"I'm too big a sinner."

"He loves you."

"Yeah, right!"

"Listen, he died for you! If there had been no one else in the whole world that needed dying for but you, he still would have come and given his life to save you. He made a way to forgive all of us, and all of us are sinners. It's just that some of us are *forgiven* sinners, and some of us are *unforgiven* sinners."

"What do I do then?" he asked.

"If you're sorry, ask him to forgive what you've done."

Then the tears came, and down on our knees we went under the cynical eyes of the policeman standing stoically in the corner of the cell.

"Will you come tomorrow?" he asked quietly, knowing the answer.

"I'm sorry, they won't let me."

"Right."

"But God will come. Morning by morning, you'll see." I left a Bible with the policeman at the desk and asked him to make sure that the young man received it. In the flyleaf I wrote, "'It is of the Lord's mercies that we are not consumed, because his compassions fail not. They are new every morning: great is thy faithfulness' (Lamentations 3:22-23). This is the way he will come to you. This is the way he'll speak to you. Love in Him, Jill—just another forgiven sinner."

As I was writing the words, another policeman appeared and said, "The superintendent wants to see you." I found myself walking down the corridor and then looking into the calculating eyes of the chief of police sitting behind his big oak desk.

"What are you doing trying to reform lost causes like this?" he asked me with a real edge to his voice.

"We're all lost causes!"

"Look, you stick to your schoolteaching and let us do our job, okay? Consider yourself a regular Florence Nightingale, don't you? This kid's got a list of crimes against him that will put him away for life, but *you* believe in him," he sneered. "How old are you?"

"Twenty-two," I replied.

"That's impressive! And this is your first job as a schoolteacher—wet behind the ears and out to change the world!"

"I believe in God," I whispered, not daring to look up. "And God's out to change the world by changing people from the inside out. It doesn't matter who we are or what we do—he'll forgive us if we ask him to. But that doesn't mean we haven't to answer for what we've done," I added hastily.

The chief dismissed me curtly with: "Well, this one's on the inside looking out now, and that's the end of him. He won't be worrying good people anymore. You don't know what you're dealing with. He's a hard nut: rape and battery, thieving, and the like."

"God loves him," I repeated stubbornly. "No one is a lost cause!"

Then I was outside the police station feeling silly, inadequate, insecure, and far, far too young. It was a miserable feeling. I drove home on my motor scooter feeling like a spanked kid.

The next day the chief called my house. My dad looked at me curiously as he handed me the phone. He wasn't too happy about my volunteer church work with teenagers. "Come in and see me," the chief ordered. I went.

"Sit down," he said. I sat, expecting more scolding.

"So you think God has forgiven him, do you?"

"Yes," I said loudly and clearly.

"Then I suppose you think he can forgive anyone."

"Yes, anyone—you, me, and everybody else." And then with my heart in my mouth, "All have sinned and come short of God's standard." My heart began to thump.

"So you think we're all sinners, do you, even police officers? Even the chief of police? Just the same as criminals, are we?" And then my heart was racing, and I was just about to change some of the message and water it down when the Spirit said loudly in my ear, *Do not omit a word.*

But the devil whispered in my other ear: *He'll throw you out, laugh at you. He'll tell your father!*

Don't be afraid. I am with you and will take care of you, said God cheerfully in both of my ears! And that was the end of it! I didn't want to offend the man, but I knew I had to deliver the whole message, and that couldn't stop with "God loves you." Why was it so much harder to tell the policeman that he was a sinner and needed Jesus than it was to tell the kid? Taking a deep breath, I told him everything God told me.

"We're all sinners for whom Christ died," I finished breathlessly. I didn't dare look at him but fixed my eyes on a spot on the floor and prayed and prayed. There was a long silence. Then quietly the police chief asked, "Tell me, young lady, what do I have to do? How does it work?"

I couldn't believe my ears. I looked up at him, and then there was no doubt. The Word had done its wonderful work. It had its own peculiar power. I had done my part by delivering it; now I had no doubt that God would do his part bringing life.

We eventually knelt down at the side of the huge oak desk with pictures of stern-looking police officers staring down at us from the stark white walls. For the second time in two days, a prodigal came home!

It doesn't matter whether we are policemen, schoolteachers, or delinquents—"All have sinned and fall short of the glory of God" (Romans 3:23). But all can come to Christ and find forgiveness. It doesn't matter whether we are shepherds, young prophets, or someone like Moses—a fugitive, albeit a forgiven fugitive, hiding in the desert. God is into using the weak and the willing. After the incident with the policeman I gained courage and prayed for strength to speak God's truth faithfully all the days of my life.

WHEN GOD'S WORD "HAPPENS" TO YOU

The Lord first gave messages to Jeremiah during the reign of Josiah when Jeremiah was about eighteen years old. He continued to give Jeremiah messages until the people were taken away into captivity. That was a period of about forty years. That's quite a testimony! Many of us in giving our own testimony may say, "The Lord spoke to me when I was in my twenties." How many of us could go on to say, "And he has continued to speak to me and give me messages for other people all my life."

In his own words Jeremiah testifies, "The word of the Lord came to me" (Jeremiah 1:4). As I noted previously, "came to" means literally "happened to." Think about it. The word of the Lord continued to "happen to" Jeremiah for over forty years. That's a lot of "happenings"!

And what "happened" to Jeremiah when the word of the Lord "opened" to him? It became a living reality within him. God's word made things happen, but it was also a happening in itself. The word of God gripped him, possessed him. It had an almost indescribable power over him.

Does this describe your experience as you have your morning devotions? Or is this just for the Jeremiahs of the world? No, it's for you and me—all who know the Lord and would make him known.

His Word Is like a Hammer

The word of God broke Jeremiah's heart. He described God's word as "like a hammer that breaks a rock in pieces" (Jeremiah 23:29). It made him stagger like a drunken man. "My heart is broken within me; all my bones tremble. I am like a drunken man, like a man overcome by wine, because of the Lord and his holy words" (Jeremiah 23:9). Well before God's word ever touched other people's lives, it touched Jeremiah. It made him tremble and stagger like a drunken man, and it broke his heart.

Have you ever had the experience of God's Word hammering away at your conscience? I have. When I first came to the States, I resisted getting involved with the women's work at church. I didn't particularly enjoy women and much preferred working with teenagers. However, God does not allow us to choose to work with those we much prefer! He wanted me to work with women. It was one of those secondary callings he had in mind for me.

I reluctantly answered an invitation to go to Memphis, Tennessee, and speak at a womens retreat. I had no other reason to go than that Stuart knew of the work and encouraged me to go.

A wonderful woman who loved working with women led the retreat. *Just my luck,* I thought to myself, watching her surreptitiously. *She's going to know I don't want to be here.* I was right. She did know because my attitude was showing. Those bad attitudes always peek beneath our behavior like a slip hanging beneath a dress. She spoke to me at the end of the conference. "You are a good speaker technically, Jill, but it's obvious you don't like women!"

"Ouch!" I replied. "You're right, and what's more I've no intention of liking them because if I do, I'm afraid God will just give me a whole lot more of them to like!"

I was really disturbed about that incident. When I got home, I spent some time with God and dared to ask him to speak to me from his Word about it. A word from Lamentations "came to" or "happened to" me that night: "Mine eye affecteth mine heart because of all the daughters of my city," lamented Jeremiah (Lamentations 3:51, KJV). Here was a man lamenting over women, while this woman—me—cared little about her own kind. Jeremiah's heart was broken for the daughters of Jerusalem and their grim state. Mine was not. But I could give God permission to take the hammer of his Word and break my heart as well. And that is exactly what I did that night!

I prayed that God would let "my eye" affect "my heart" when I looked at the women of my city, that I would feel and see what he felt and saw, and that I would do everything I could to reach them. The release was palpable, and I began fulfilling one of my secondary callings that day. Starting with six women in a home investigative Bible study, God gave me a heart for women that has resulted in reaching thousands of women around the world with his Word.

All he wants is for you to say, "Break my heart, God," and he will. He will use the hammer of his Word on the anvil of your life, and you will find Jeremiah's experience to be yours. "My eyes fail from weeping, I am in torment within, my heart is poured out on the ground because my people are destroyed" (Lamentations 2:11). If God's Word dwells in us richly hour by hour, we will live and work with a broken heart—and it will show.

His Word Is like a Fire

God told Jeremiah that his Word that hammered home the truth could also be described as a fire. "Is not my word like fire?" asks the Lord (Jeremiah 23:29).

As Jeremiah began faithfully preaching the words God gave him, he ran into a whole lot of trouble. The people didn't want a "God-happening" in their lives. When the word that had "happened to"

Jeremiah "happened through" Jeremiah to the people of Israel, they not only rejected it, they rejected the one who delivered it as well. "The word of the Lord has brought me insult and reproach all day long. But if I say, 'I will not mention him or speak any more in his name,' his word is in my heart like a fire, a fire shut up in my bones. I am weary of holding it in; indeed, I cannot" (Jeremiah 20:8-9). When the Word happens to us, it "fires us up," and we cannot contain it even if it brings us a whole lot of trouble.

So how exactly does this word come to us? How did the word of the Lord come to Jeremiah? Did he hear a human voice? Did he fall into a deep sleep and have a dream? I don't think God spoke to Jeremiah in a dream because in chapter 23 the Lord tells Jeremiah what he thinks about the dreams of the false prophets. Listen to what God says: "I have heard what the prophets say who prophesy lies in my name. They say, 'I had a dream! I had a dream!' How long will this continue in the hearts of these lying prophets, who prophesy the delusions of their own minds? . . . Let the prophet who has a dream tell his dream, but let the one who has my word speak it faithfully" (Jeremiah 23:25-26, 28). And then again, "'I am against the prophets who wag their own tongues and yet declare, "The Lord declares." Indeed, I am against those who prophesy false dreams,' declares the Lord. 'They tell them and lead my people astray with their reckless lies, yet I did not send or appoint them. They do not benefit these people in the least'" (Jeremiah 23:31-32).

The word that truly comes from God benefits people because it doesn't hide the unpalatable truth. So even though God certainly used dreams to speak to people in Old Testament times, there were God-given dreams and false dreams. In Jeremiah's case it seems that God spoke to him directly. The Lord used words to instruct Jeremiah to tell the people his messages. Jeremiah was to say, "Thus says the Lord," not "I had a dream."

We don't know exactly what the word of the Lord sounded like to the prophet, but we do know what it did to him. It shattered his heart and fired him up. When God truly speaks, his word is invested with self-existent power able to transform what it touches. The recipients become so sure of its truth that they let it do its life-shattering, transforming work. Then they find themselves ignited with the fire of God. They are driven to open their mouths and let it "happen" to others, or they "burn up" trying to contain it.

For those of us living today, the word of the Lord has been written down. We don't have to rely on dreams or voices from the heavens. We don't have to "steal from one another words supposedly from" God (Jeremiah 23:30). We can read the Bible for ourselves and relay it to others. Remember that only a few could read in Jeremiah's day; they had to be content with having others read to them. But today in the West, very nearly all of us can read, and the infallible Word of God is our reliable document for all matters of faith and doctrine.

The New Testament confirms this: "All Scripture is God-breathed and is useful for teaching, rebuking, correcting and training in righteousness, so that the man of God may be thoroughly equipped for every good work" (2 Timothy 3:16-17). As we read the written Word, it should make our knees tremble. It should break our hearts. It should benefit its hearers and light a fire under us so that as it "happens" to us, it drives us on until it "happens" to others. We need to let the written Word do its own dynamic work in us, to us, and through us. When you read the written Word of God, do you believe what it tells you about itself? That it is, indeed, the Word of God to you today? Does it come dynamically to you each time you read it so that you can never be the same again?

Perhaps it came to you once with the kind of power I have been describing, but now that reality is like a dream in itself. You can hardly remember what it was like when the Word "happened" to you last. Let me ask you a question: What happened to what "happened"? If someone was writing down your experiences over years of being a Bible-believing Christian and asked you, "What happened to what 'happened'?" what would you say?

Let me encourage you from my own experience. There have been times in my life when I have not allowed the Word to break my heart. I have read the Bible with others in mind and avoided the painful practice of letting the Word refine me like a fire. To use another picture, God has fed me with bread from heaven, but I have not cleaned up my plate. Too many times I have lost my appetite, and the Word has been neither my delight nor my desire. But God has always been faithful to face me with my spiritual anorexia and set me off collecting my daily manna morning by morning again. It is never too late to start again, for "his compassions never fail. They are new every morning" (Lamentations 3:22-23).

His Word Is like Bread

So what do we do when God makes his Word available to us? We eat it! "When your words came, I ate them; they were my joy and my heart's delight" (Jeremiah 15:16). Are his words your joy and your heart's delight, or are they distasteful? Do you read your daily Scripture portion impatiently, going through the motions with your mind on other things, or do you delight in your time "in the garden of your soul"? Life outside Eden can present you with so many thorny problems! So life in the garden is doubly important. It is here you are to walk with him and talk with him. It is here you share your deepest fears and realize your most daring dreams. And it is here that he shares with you his heart.

These words of God are, as Jesus said, our most necessary food. We are to live life outside the garden by them. We are to live "on every word that comes from the mouth of God" (Matthew 4:4). As the children of Israel collected the manna from heaven every day for forty years, so we are to collect our bread from heaven on a daily basis as well.

We are to take whatever time it takes to collect it, and we are also to take time to eat and digest it properly. That usually means that we need to take time to meditate on his Word. *Meditate* means "to chew something over, to digest its meaning, to think about it long enough for it to nourish our souls." The problem so often is that we, in true Western fashion, "grab a bite." We do not graze in the green pastures but merely grab a blade of grass as we charge out the door into our far too busy days. I promise you, you will not get indigestion if you eat the Bread of Life slowly and carefully enough. When we eat as God intends us to eat, we will find that the Bread of Life is like honey from the honeycomb, both a joy and a delight. "They are sweeter than honey, than honey from the comb," says Psalm 19:10. God instructed Joshua, "Do not let this Book of the Law depart from your mouth; meditate on it day and night, so that you may be careful to do everything written in it" (Joshua 1:8). As we meditate on God's Word, we obtain nourishment for our souls.

But what do we do when meditating on Scripture is not a joy or a delight? What do we do when it tastes bitter? We are to eat it anyway. Whether it breaks or delights our hearts, we are to eat it, digest it, and put it to good use.

The prophet John had this experience. An angel brought him the word of God written on a scroll and told him to eat it. He did, and it tasted like honey but gave him a stomachache! He had bitter words for the people, for the angel told him, "You must prophesy again about many peoples, nations, languages and kings" (Revelation 10:11).

Sometimes that will be our experience as well. We will not always find God's Word soothing and comforting and making us feel good. Sometimes he will bring a word of rebuke or prepare us for some bad news that we will have to swallow. We may be left with a very bitter taste in our mouths. At other times it will be a bitter message for someone else to whom God wants us to speak. We need to be in the daily habit of eating whatever God puts in front of us, however palatable or unpalatable.

Purchase a good reference Bible if you do not have one. The Bible is its own best interpreter, and one reference leads to the next so that the words are clarified and you can understand them better. Get a Bible guide, and read the Bible through systematically. Discipline yourself to read it every day. Start to read, mark, and inwardly digest the Scriptures. See what God will start to do to you, in you, and through you.

When I began to eat the spiritual food God had prepared for me,

I found it first a joy and then a challenge. The ongoing challenge was to be as thoroughly thrilled with any and all food he chose for me. It was a joy and delight to find a word that assured me of my salvation. That was sweet, but I also found a word that assured me that those I loved were lost without Christ. That was harder to swallow and digest. But we cannot pick and choose which words we will eat and which we will leave on the side of our plate because we do not like them.

As a grandmother of thirteen I often hear myself telling one of my grandchildren, "Clean up your plate." If I expect the children to eat everything, I know it is very important for the children to see my own plate clean. As I model my clear delight in all the food that is provided, those around who are watching may find a growing appetite for a balanced diet themselves. As we learn to "clean up our plates," we will be nourished accordingly and will grow to be balanced lovers and students of the Word.

SPEAKING THE TRUTH OF GOD'S WORD

As we receive both the Word that is a joy and the Word that is a challenge, we need to pass on both the Word that delights and the Word that directs. The false prophets were masters at passing on only the pleasant word, the soothing word. In fact, they passed along only words the people wanted to hear, not what they needed to hear: " 'Peace, peace,' they say, when there is no peace" (Jeremiah 6:14). This was not so of Jeremiah. Surely he was tempted at times to pick and choose the messages he passed along to the people. But God reminded him of his mandate one day when he was about to deliver a particularly strong message in the temple: "Tell them everything I command you; do not omit a word," warned the Lord (Jeremiah 26:2). *The New English Bible* renders this: "You shall tell them everything that I command you to say to them, keeping nothing back."

The word *omit* is interesting. The same Hebrew word is also used in Isaiah 15:2 to describe the clipping of a beard, or shaving off a piece of something. "Every head is shaved and every beard cut off."

How descriptive. God was warning Jeremiah not to "clip off" any of the words he had instructed Jeremiah to say!

Now I can certainly relate to that! How often I have been talking to a stranger on a plane and told that person only that portion of the Word of God that was a joy and delight to tell. Yet I've been aware of the still small voice urging me to share the bad news as well as the good news.

Once a man I was talking to seemed to be really interested in the gospel. As I talked to him, the voice of God kept whispering in my soul's ear, *When are you going to tell him about hell?*

Not yet, Lord, I whispered back. *It would put him off.*

Back came the answer: *You must go to everyone I tell you to and tell them everything I tell you to. Do not omit a word!*

I was so tempted to clip off some of the message. However, I took a deep breath and introduced the subject into the conversation. He looked at me in amazement and said, "I can't remember having met anyone in this day and age who actually believes in a hell. They don't believe in hell in my subdivision!" He was a little irritated with me from that point on, but I felt relieved in my spirit for not "omitting" or "shaving off" any of the message.

At least I was not subjected to the same treatment as Jeremiah was when he was careful not to "omit" a word. "As soon as Jeremiah finished telling all the people everything the Lord had commanded him to say, the priests, the prophets and all the people seized him and said, 'You must die!'" (Jeremiah 26:8). Of course, we hope that this will not be the result at the end of your conversations! In fact, it is very unlikely that you will face such treatment in your country. But you may well lose friends or family by faithfully passing on the truth of God's Word to them. Fear of that possibility makes it easy to get out those beard clippers and shave away.

God's Word and Your Pen (or Computer!)

Baruch had the same temptations as Jeremiah. He was called to pass on the word of the Lord as surely as the prophet was. His pen would relay God's words to his own family, who were in the leadership of

Israel, as well as to all the people. Baruch wrote God's messages faithfully on his scroll with ink and tried not to "omit" a word. (See Jeremiah 36:17-18.)

Baruch was first and foremost a scribe. He knew the power of the word of God and was as intent on getting people to read it as Jeremiah was on getting people to hear it. He was not like the other scribes. Jeremiah said: "How can you say, 'We are wise, for we have the law of the Lord,' when actually the lying pen of the scribes has handled it falsely?" (Jeremiah 8:8). One time Jeremiah was under house arrest, and Baruch had to go to the temple and read God's messages to the people himself. It must have been very tempting for him to get his clippers out when he came to the uncomplimentary bits about his relatives! But he, like Jeremiah, was faithful and read every last word.

When I came to Christ at college, I began to lead people to the Lord. At the end of the term I returned home for the break. Concerned about keeping the new believers believing, I began to write to them. I became a scribe for God! I discovered that the written word could be even more effective than the spoken word. If I wrote a letter, I could read it over and see if it was really what I wanted to say. And if it wasn't, I could do it again and get it right. I could also keep a copy and remember what I'd said. My ministry of letter writing burgeoned until I was spending most of my spare time writing to encourage the new converts. This is something you may think about—a ministry of letter writing. It's a great way to get God's Word on your paper and then into people's hands and hearts.

We can buy someone else's words and give them to people, too. I can't tell you how much books meant to me as a young Christian. Knowing how they helped me, I started to buy Christian books and send them to fellow students I wanted to influence for the Lord. There are dozens of ways you can be a Jeremiah or a Baruch and get the word out.

As I grew in my faith, I was invited to write my own books. What a privilege to be asked to write a book of my own! This was yet one more way God could use me to get his Word into the hands of those who needed it. At first I felt like Jeremiah. I was too young. I had never been trained as a writer. I didn't type, and so it took me a long time to write out everything. However, I recognized that I should not turn down the opportunity, so I began.

I wrote my first book in 1975. God's words were on my pages, and the book sold well. I was asked to do another book and then another. As I traveled, I wrote. I wrote everywhere. I took up my pen in airports, restaurants, hotels, and people's homes. In my own kitchen, living room, and bedroom I put words down on paper. The publishers eventually sorted them out, and the books kept coming.

After forty-five books and a lot of years, I faced a new challenge: "Learn to type, Mother," advised my computer-savvy daughter. Indeed, all my family kept after me. But I was totally intimidated at the thought. This time I didn't say, "I'm too young," but rather, "I'm too old!" After all, I was sixty-five years old and felt it was too late to learn another skill. I had always had a long-suffering secretary who would gather my scribbled notes and arrange them beautifully on her typewriter and later on her computer, writing my manuscript for me. She was a wonderful "Baruch." But I realized I would produce better work, and maybe more material, if I could learn to type and master the computer myself.

This was one of the greatest challenges of my life! But the motivation was the fact that people were still asking me for teaching material and there was no way I could respond if I didn't bite the bullet and move into the computer age.

As I began to study and then teach this material on Baruch and Jeremiah and was asked to put it into book form, I said to the Lord, "I could get this done so much quicker if I only could use the computer. Help me to be a good scribe and learn a new skill, even at my age."

My grandchildren gazed at me with wide, solemn eyes when I told the family I was going to join the twenty-first century. "We'll help you, Nana," promised our ten-year-old Christy. Ty, at fourteen, was a whiz at all the technical things that seemed such a total mystery to me and gave me a good start by teaching me simple skills. The grandchildren all helped, and so did our daughter-in-law, who is our ministry assistant. She, along with our daughter, became my cheering section. Christy gave me her typing rules from school. "I've finished with them a long time ago, Nana," she assured me! It was humiliating but fun. The greatest test came when Judy's five-year-old, Stephen, invited me into the computer room at their house for a lesson. Watching him "boot up" his computer and deftly press a bewildering array of buttons made me feel like Methuselah, but I stuck with it. Turning around to face me, he lifted the mouse and showed it to me. "Nana," he said, "this is a mouse!" Swallowing my pride, I nodded humbly and settled down to my lesson. Somehow I achieved my goal, and I began to type my book. This is now the second book I have written on a computer.

So it may be "his words in my mouth," or "his words in my letters or on a pretty card," or "his words on my computer." One way or another, God helping me, I am determined to get his Word out to as many people as I can.

You can do the same. Maybe you will never write a book, but you could buy someone else's book or purchase pretty cards and write encouraging notes to people who need them. Perhaps you will never be a speaker, but you could send other people's words on a tape or over the Internet.

As I am writing these words, I have just come to New Zealand from Australia. While "down under," I was reminded of the amazing story of the man who spent his life writing one word on the pavements of Sydney. That one word was *eternity*. Over this man's lifetime he scribbled that word in chalk all over the city's pavements. God used it to alert thousands of people to eternal things. At the winter Olympics that one word was displayed over the Sidney harbor bridge so that all the world could see it. It is now considered part of the culture and history of Sydney! Surely, like this man, we could all manage to think of a way to write, tell, send, or pass on at least one word from the Lord!

God's Word to Your Family and Friends

Baruch was a skilled scribe, but that didn't mean he always got a hearing. His own family members were not all convinced by his skilled pen, but then sometimes our family and friends are the hardest people to tell about the Lord. I faced this challenge as soon as I became a Christian.

Converted at Cambridge, I found the biggest challenge to my faith waiting for me back home in Liverpool at semester break. Thinking about a plan of attack as I rode the train back from college, I decided to get it all over in one fell swoop. I sent out invitations to my six closest friends for a coming-home party and wondered if they would show up. They did. I had left the invitation somewhat ambiguous, saying that I wanted to tell them about a wonderful event in my life. They knew me well, and I knew they would think that I had fallen in love and gotten engaged!

They arrived at my party clutching engagement presents and eagerly waiting for the news. I remember looking at them in wonder and thinking, *Now which bit do I tell them first?* Needless to say, I had my beard clippers ready! After stumbling around the subject, I burned my bridges and told them I had fallen in love with God and I wanted them all to do the same.

There was total silence at the end of my garbled speech. Looking around, I realized there was going to be a cost involved in this Christianity. It was a heavy cost for me—all but one of those good friends left my life as they left the house that night. One friend stayed to hear more and accepted the Lord. Not long ago, forty years later, she wrote to thank me for not "omitting" a word that night.

The experiences I have had in speaking and teaching over my forty years of ministry—whether to individuals, groups, or audiences small or great—make me realize that the words in my mouth have been God's words. The message I have relayed has been the Word of God that I have hidden in my heart and memorized over the years. It has not been my own bright ideas that have convinced street kids to stop taking drugs. It has not been the educated guess or some psychological theory that has changed lives. It has been the Word of God given out in the power of the Spirit that has worked the miracle of transformation in people's lives.

God has been faithful to put his words in my mouth when I have faced the biggest challenges of my life. One day during the Bosnia-Croatian-Serbian conflict, I found myself in Osiek on the border of Croatia and Bosnia. There was a seminary there, and I was working with a relief agency at the refugee center based in that seminary. The president of the seminary was Dr. Peter Kuzmic. All day we processed refugees who were streaming over the border; in the evenings Dr. Kuzmic and his students would lead a church service for the incoming men, women, and children.

One evening as we were getting ready for the service, there was an explosion. The church belonging to the only Serb priest left in that Croatian town was blown up. Dr. Kuzmic said to me, "Jill, I have to go to the man and his wife with the mayor and police and see if we can salvage any of this poor man's goods. You speak to the people for me." Can you imagine how I felt about that? What would you have said to those people? How could I say anything to them? I could not relate to their dilemma. I had never been a refugee. I complained to the Lord about this, to which he replied, *I have. I have been a refugee.*

When was Jesus a refugee, I wondered? And then I remembered. He had been a refugee when he was a baby and Herod's soldiers had come to Bethlehem to kill him. *I am not asking you to tell them your story,* said the Lord. *I am asking you to tell them mine.* And then Jeremiah's words popped into my head: "You must go to everyone I send you to and say whatever I command you. . . . Then the Lord reached out his hand and touched my mouth and said to me, 'Now, I have put my words in your mouth'" (Jeremiah 1:7, 9).

I can remember climbing up into that high pulpit in the seminary church and praying, *Your words in my mouth, Lord. Your words in my mouth.* And he was as true to his word to me as he had been to Jeremiah. As I spoke, he spoke. I passed on his message, not mine. I told those people what he said, what he thought about the terrible things that had happened to them, and how he wanted them to turn to him for healing and help and salvation. And his word was effective and "happened to" them, changing some of those people forever.

He has put "his words in my mouth." In the measure that I have been faithful to speak it out, God has honored his Word as he promised to do. "As the rain and snow come down from heaven, and do not return to it without watering the earth and making it bud and flourish, so that it yields seed for the sower and bread for the eater, so is my word that goes out from my mouth: It will not return to me empty, but will accomplish what I desire and achieve the purpose for which I sent it" (Isaiah 55:10-11). Thus says the Lord!

Chiseled by the Word of God that happened to my heart
Shattered by the truth I know you want me to impart
Broken by the Word of power that had first broken me
Drawn by the fire of God to speak and set it free.

TIME OUT

These worksheets can be used in groups, in church classes, or with individuals as a discipling tool. They can also be used in a personal quiet time.

Take Time

1. Read Acts 1:5 and 5:20-42. What does the incident from Acts 5 teach about the way God gets his Word out today?
2. Paul and Jeremiah had many similar experiences. Read the following references, and compare these two men's reactions to the call of God. What does that mean for us today?

   • Acts 18:9-10
   • Titus 2:15

3. God's Word is like a hammer, a fire, and bread. Which figure of speech speaks to you and why?
4. Suggest other similes for the Word of God that mirror your own experience. (For example, "The Word of God is like a measuring stick.") Explain how this picture applies to you.
5. Discuss other ways we could get the Word of God out today.
6. What do you think hinders us from doing this?

Prayer Time

1. Praise God for trusting us with his Word.
2. Thank God for putting his words in our mouths.
3. Ask God to bless Christian educators and the children they teach.
4. Pray for a good reception for the ministry of missionaries.
5. Pray for your own family.

A Letter to God

Write a letter to God asking him to put his words in your mouth.

CHAPTER SIX

Faith in God's Refreshment

<hr>

Your Roots in His River

Blessed is the man who trusts in the Lord,
whose confidence is in him. He will be like
a tree planted by the water that sends
out its roots by the stream.
JEREMIAH 17:7-8

A FRIEND OF OURS WAS TRAVELING ON A TRAIN IN ENGLAND.
He was reading a book when the gentleman in the opposite corner
said to him, "Excuse me, young man, but you seem to have found the
secret of life!" Our friend was momentarily taken aback. After all, he
had been unaware anyone was watching him, and all he had been doing
was reading a book! He quickly recovered himself and with a broad
smile said, "Well, sir, I have no idea what made you say that, but I suppose if I were to tell you I have found the secret of life and what that secret is, I would have to tell you I have 'my roots in the river'!" The man
looked mystified, but our friend had the time on that journey to explain
what he meant. He told him all about life in the Spirit.

We will never finish strong unless we understand what it means
to have our roots in the river of God. Life in the Spirit means our
faith is freshened by the water of life moment by moment and day
by day until our confidence and trust in God are so obvious that
even total strangers will notice and comment on them.

ROOTS IN THE RIVER

Jeremiah had a wonderful way of using pictures to illustrate spiritual truths. Here in the middle of some pretty dire predictions and
depressing news he throws in a little parable of life and hope.

God is first and foremost interested in *how* we are doing and not in *what* we are doing—in the *person*, not the *performance*. God wanted Jeremiah to do well spiritually, whatever the results of his ministry. He wanted him to endure life's adversities without anxiety and to help others do the same. That's what he wants us all to do. He wants us to live life planted in the stream of the Spirit, weathering the weather and being fresh, fruitful, and faithful.

The figure is graphic. Here is a tree, impervious to heat and drought, doing what it was created to do. Its boughs are full of sap, its leaves are ever green, and its branches are full of fruit for the picking and enjoyment of all who pass by. This is a wonderful picture of what the Bible calls "life in the Spirit."

I was eighteen before I began to understand who the Holy Spirit was. I had heard about the Holy Ghost as we said the creed in assembly in our school every day. "I believe in the Holy Ghost," I had intoned along with hundreds of other schoolgirls, having no clue about anything I was reciting. If I had given the subject any thought at all, I imagined a sort of sheet-shrouded ghost haunting old English graveyards! Only after becoming a Christian did I learn that the Holy Ghost (the Holy Spirit) is the third person of the Trinity, equal with God because he is God.

The Bible describes him in many ways: oil, wind, water, and fire, to mention just a few. These symbols are figures of speech that illustrate his person and work.

The symbol of water to describe the person and work of the Spirit has been particularly meaningful to me. Maybe that is because even at the age of eighteen I was parched and dry, having drunk at broken springs of water that did not satisfy me. As I began to study the Scriptures, I noticed that blessing, fertility, and water are used almost interchangeably in the Old and New Testaments.

Jesus said to the woman at the well of Sychar, "If you knew the gift of God and who it is that asks you for a drink, you would have asked him and he would have given you living water" (John 4:10). This woman had been drinking at the river of her relationships. She had had five husbands, and the man she was living with when Jesus spoke to her was not her husband. Jesus offered her a spiritual experience that would quench her thirst—a relationship with the living God.

A few days later at a feast day, Jesus used this picture again. In the middle of a ritual when the priests carried in a large jar of water and poured it out, Jesus got up and cried out with a loud voice, "'Whoever believes in me, as the Scripture has said, streams of living water will flow from within him.' By this he meant the Spirit, whom those who believed in him were later to receive" (John 7:38-39). What a claim, that "he who believes in me will never be thirsty" (John 6:35). Only God could claim such a thing. Jesus is God and therefore is able to offer this soul-saving water of life to all who ask him for the gift.

Another picture of water in the Bible is that of the river of life. Ezekiel vividly describes the fruit trees that line its banks and the river of life flowing from the throne of God:

> I saw a great number of trees on each side of the river. . . . Fruit trees of all kinds will grow on both banks of the river. Their leaves will not wither, nor will their fruit fail. Every month they will bear, because the water from the sanctuary flows to them. Their fruit will serve for food and their leaves for healing. (Ezekiel 47:7, 12)

There is no doubt that this river was the same river Jeremiah had in mind in chapter 17, and incidentally, the same river the apostle John saw years later in his vision on the island of Patmos. John said,

> Then the angel showed me the river of the water of life, as clear as crystal, flowing from the throne of God and of the Lamb down the middle of the great street of the city. On each side of the river stood the tree of life, bearing twelve crops of fruit, yielding its fruit every month. And the leaves of the tree are for the healing of the nations. (Revelation 22:1-2)

The source of the river is God himself. Ezekiel observed that everything that touched the river lived, and, in fact, wherever the river flowed, there was life. There were many trees growing on the sides of this river; the leaves of these trees never turned brown or fell, and there was always fruit on their branches.

Ever since I saw this figure in Scripture, I wanted that experience. How could I send out my roots by this wonderful river? How could my life be ever green and laden down with the fruit of the Spirit? It is not my responsibility to produce the fruit of the Spirit but to make sure I allow God room to produce that fruit in my life. The tree was planted by the river, but it had to send out "its roots by the stream" (Jeremiah 17:8). This "sending out roots" was my part. I realized soon after giving my life to Christ that I had the frightening choice about into which river I put my roots.

RIVERS THAT CANNOT QUENCH YOUR THIRST

The River of Relationships

Many rivers of experience are available to us. One of the widest is the river of relationships. As a teenager I had put my roots into the river of relationships and had come up dry. Even after coming to faith, I had looked for satisfaction in my relationships with others before looking to God for fulfillment.

After my conversion to Christ, a man came into my life who didn't know the Lord. He was kind and successful, and he loved me. He had no interest, however, in the things of God. I knew the Bible was unequivocal on the subject. I read in Deuteronomy 29:23 that because of disobedience, the children of Israel would experience life on the salt flats, where there would be "nothing planted, nothing sprouting, no vegetation growing on it." The land would be reduced to "a burning waste of salt and sulfur." The people of God brought this calamity on their nation and themselves because they put their roots down into the wrong rivers—in particular, the river of wrong relationships. God had expressly forbidden his people to make close relationships with the people around them lest their gods steal their hearts away from the Lord. They had disobeyed his repeated warnings in this regard and as a result were barren and useless.

As I pursued this relationship with this man who did not know the Lord, I noticed there was "nothing growing, nothing sprouting" in my life, and I knew why. If we put our roots down into forbidden relationships as the people of God did in the history of Israel, our leaves will wither and turn brown, and there will certainly be no fruit on our branches. My roots had to be extracted from this river and put down into the one relationship that mattered, and that was with God through his Son Jesus Christ by his Spirit.

The River of Religion

Where are your roots? Are they deep in the river of a relationship or perhaps in the river of religion? A form of religion without reality is a miserable affair. Paul warns us that in the last days there will be people around who will be "lovers of pleasure rather than lovers of God—having a form of godliness but denying its power." Paul writes that we are to have "nothing to do with them" (2 Timothy 3:4-5).

There is a broad river of religion that flows throughout the world, and many put out their roots by that stream. Jesus said there was only one way to the Father, and that was through him. "No one comes to the Father except through me," he told us (John 14:6). All other paths will turn out to be salt flats and burning sulfur.

Perhaps the most prevalent religion of all is the worship of self. Jeremiah warns about this. "Cursed is the one who trusts in man, who depends on flesh for his strength. . . . He will be like a bush in the wastelands" (Jeremiah 17:5-6). Our selfish self boasts, "I can do anything I want to do, and I don't need anyone to help me to do it." The core of real Christianity is dependence, not self-reliance. The problem is that Christians don't find themselves free from this battle between self and Spirit once they come to faith. If we put confidence in the flesh, we will finish up dry and desperate. The measure of our maturity in God is in self-forgetfulness and not self-reliance.

The more mature the tree, the less self-reliant it will be. The bigger it gets, the more roots it will put out.

Looking after my grandchildren one day, I was amused at their total self-absorption. It was cute. It will not be cute, however, when they become young adults! When we see to it that our roots are in the river of spirituality and not the river of self, our lives will be productive and delightful.

The river of self-reliance looks very similar to the river of life. We can be tricked into thinking, *I can do this,* whatever "this" is. Even after being in Christian ministry for a long time, I have caught myself drawing from this false river of the flesh. I was somewhat comforted to find that other speakers have had the same battle. For instance, the well-known preacher G. Campbell Morgan once said that one day after preaching for many years he found himself relying on himself and his own expertise and not on the Spirit. He said, "It is possible to be homiletically brilliant, verbally fluent, theologically profound, biblically accurate, and spiritually useless. That frightens me, my brothers and sisters. I hope it frightens you too."

It's very sobering to be caught up only in homiletical ability, fluency, theological profundity, and biblical accuracy, only to have God say, "Preach on, great preacher—without me." On this occasion, G. Campbell Morgan said that he feared that those were God's words to him.

The river of religion—the religion of self, of self-reliance, or even of doctrine—does not satisfy. You will find yourself facing only drought.

TIMES OF DROUGHT

Jeremiah contrasts the tree on the bank of the flowing stream with a bush in the wastelands. This bush is just a little scrub bush that sits in the sun and burns up "in a salt land where no one lives" (Jeremiah 17:6). This is not to say there were no other scrub bushes around; it was just that no bush "lived" there—*really* lived there. You may be a scrub-bush person surrounded by hundreds of other scrub bushes but feel as lonely as if you were absolutely on your own in the desert. It is not pleasant to be a scrub bush in the wastelands.

It is possible to be a Christian and yet feel as isolated and cut off from anything fresh and living as the scrub bush in the wastelands. I have met such little scrub bushes in the far corners of the world as well as in North America. Do you feel as if I am describing you? Let me ask you some questions.

Do you ever go to church and feel lonely even though you are in a crowd? Do you look around at your Christian friends and find that they are all as dead and dry as you feel? Above all, do you feel alone?

One characteristic of life in the Spirit is the consciousness of the presence of God so you never feel alone. As you live life in the Spirit, you might be alone physically, but you will never be lonely spiritually—and there is a difference. Jeremiah certainly felt alone. He was abandoned by his family and his people, but he wrote about an experience of obedience in his relationship with God that led to his roots' being in the river of life. He discovered that God was nearer than breathing, closer than hands and feet. He was a person who had no worries in a year of relational drought.

Perhaps you have had a year of drought in the area of your relationships. Oh, you might have many friends, but somehow those relationships aren't bringing what you expected. You have an intimate loneliness that no one seems to fill. Why not look at those relationships again and ask yourself a question: How is my primary relationship with God doing? Am I trying to satisfy my needs with people before developing a satisfying relationship with God? Am I developing an intimate communion with the Lord, or do I call on him only when I need something? That's a bit like the student at the university who called his father only when he wanted money!

There was a period of my life when I was single and there was no serious man on the horizon. I began to pray about this. I listened to myself and knew I was being less than honest in my prayers. *Dear Lord,* I prayed fervently, *I am willing to stay unmarried for you.* I knew in my heart that this was just not true. I was quietly hoping that God would be so impressed with my fervent prayer that he would give me a husband! Eventually I got honest and got down to business with God. What I really needed to talk about was my fear of staying single. If there was to be a lifetime drought of men in my life, how could I ever be happy? Once I had asked God to satisfy my heart with him alone, I was able to experience the presence of God in reality. I could trust that if there were not to be a man for me, then God would be my constant companion. If we cannot come to the point of being happy though single, we will never be fully happy though married, for Christians are called to be "singleminded" for the Lord (I Corinthians 7:29).

Maybe you have had a year of drought in the area of your vocation. Maybe you were released from your job or couldn't work in the area of your expertise anymore. Perhaps God has been calling you to the mission field. Again you may have been less than honest with yourself or God. You may even have been praying publicly, "Lord, I am willing to go," when you are secretly planning to stay! The tree planted by the river has no worries about leaving home and family for the foreign field. When you are planted by the river, you can see an unplanned-for change of vocation as God's way of freeing you up to move out into his plan for your life. After all, the river of life flows through every country in the whole wide world wherever God plants you!

It could be you have had a year of drought in the area of your health. There may have been an absence of concern on the part of others about your condition, or you may be suffering a debilitating chronic condition. The tree with its roots in the river draws comfort and strength from the river's source and is content despite health issues.

So has this been a year of drought for you? Perhaps your friendships shriveled or funds dried up. Maybe you got passed over for a promotion that you had waited all your life to win. It could be that you moved to a different city because of your husband's job and your marriage has taken a beating because of the move. Is your child doing poorly in school? Is the heat on for your Christian child who is getting laughed at by her schoolmates?

Or is the drought in your ministry? Do you feel like a bush in the wasteland, finding no one interested in your Sunday school lessons or in your really bright idea for the women's board? Maybe you have been depending on the flesh and coming up empty. Are you a minister of the gospel and your church has treated you unfairly and run you out of town? Are you spiritually dry, dry, dry? Take your little roots out of whatever river they are in and deliberately transfer them into the river of life. You will never regret it!

When you have experienced a year of drought in any of these areas, it is bound to bring worries into your life. But worries are drowned in the river of God! The tree planted by the river has "no worries in a year of drought" (Jeremiah 17:8) because its roots reach into the river of healing and help. That river of life provides renewed trust in the God who can give you refreshment.

AVOID THE SCRUB BUSHES

Don't look for help anywhere else but from the river or other ever green trees. If you hang around other scrub bushes too much, you could become like them. They will not be able to help you because they have problems, too. They are burning up like you are and can only think of themselves. Are your deepest friendships with scrub bushes or with green, fruitful trees? God wants you to choose your friends from among those on the riverbank who have their roots in the river, not from among scrub bushes trying to survive in the wastelands. But above all, he wants you to find your main joy in your relationship with him. Then, if you are planted in a place where the next tree lives a long way along the riverbank, you can know that if you keep your roots in the river, you will still be all right. You will have found the secret of life lived in the Spirit and joy in the fact that he "will never leave you nor forsake you" (Joshua 1:5).

Trying to find help from scrub bushes is a bit like the Prodigal Son's trying to find help from his friends in the far country. The poor guy finished up in the pigsty, and "no one gave him anything" (Luke 15:16). His fair-weather friends, his scrub-bush companions, forsook him once his money ran out.

I vividly remember giving up the young man whom I had wanted to marry but who was not a believer. It was a momentous struggle. But at last it was done. I told the Lord, "I would rather be miserable without him if it means being happy with you than be happy with him if it means being miserable without you!" Like the Prodigal Son, my friend could only give me his scrub-bush love, and it wasn't enough. I was so glad when I returned my roots to the river. Then the river flowed out of my life again, and my leaves turned green.

You have a choice to be a blessed person or a cursed one. The little scrub bush felt cursed, whereas the tree by the river felt blessed. "Cursed is the one who trusts in man, who depends on flesh for his strength and whose heart turns away from the Lord. He will be like a bush in the wastelands; he will not see prosperity when it comes. He will dwell in the parched places of the desert" (Jeremiah 17:5-6). In contrast, "Blessed is the man who trusts in the Lord, whose confidence is in him. He will be like a tree planted by the water" (Jeremiah 17:7-8).

The Christian life is not lived in a vacuum. It is lived out in those everyday decisions and choices. Whenever people saw me—a young woman happy without a neat boyfriend—they would say to me as they said to that man on the train, "Young woman, you seem to have found the secret of life!" The picture of this little tree totally fulfilled, living its life with its branches groaning under the weight of all its luscious fruit, is not a dream that can never come true. It is a reality waiting to be realized. It is up to you.

When Your Roots Are in the River

You Experience Reconciliation
There is another river that runs through our world. At its source it is called the river of reconciliation. According to Ezekiel and John, both of whom had a vision of it, it begins in the throne room of God. It is the life of the Son of God by the Spirit, the life of Jesus Christ. It is the river of redemption and the river of grace and the river of mercy all in one. It is the river of love that never fails, hope

that never quits, and compassion that goes on flowing all over us. It is a great river, an everlasting river, and a river we do not deserve. It overflows with reconciliation with God and reconciliation with each other. God breaks down the walls we build between him and ourselves and forgives us all things. Then he helps us to forgive others freely as we have been forgiven.

You will need to keep your roots in the river to allow forgiveness to flow through you to others. Forgiving others means refusing to reserve the right to vengeance. You forfeit the satisfaction of getting others back for wrongs they have done to you. You give up nursing grudges, and as much as you can, you live at peace with all people. God knows how to do that, for he has forgiven the world. Those who wish to thank him for that become good forgivers themselves. A marriage that works, for instance, is made up of two good forgivers. Those of us who are aware of just how much we have been forgiven love God very much and want to become like him in this respect.

Ask God to plant you by this river, and you will never need to transplant yourself anywhere else your entire life. Indeed, you would be foolish to do so. Just let your roots rest in the water and get on with the ministry of reconciliation, and let the world do its worst.

And what will happen if you do rest in the river and the world, the flesh, and the devil do their worst? Then you will find that God will do his best! You will discover that you are not worrying about the weather! The drought will no doubt come, but when the heat is on, you won't dry up. In fact, the drought will cause you to draw more deeply on the stream of grace and reconciliation flowing within you.

You Are Ever Green

And how will you know if this transaction has taken place? By the color of your leaves! If you look into the river to see your reflection, you will notice leaves that are ever green and healthy. A favorite verse of mine says, "The trees of the Lord are full of sap" (Psalm 104:16, KJV). I like to think of the sap as Scripture. As my roots are in the river of God and my mind is soaked in the Word of God, something sprouts. What is inside comes out. Evergreen trees ignore the seasons. When the summer heat is on or the winter winds blast, their leaves shine on. So with my roots in the river and my mind in the Word, I can shine on too. I can bring color to a drab landscape. People can find relief from the heat under my evergreen tree in the summer, and shelter from the storm in the winter. An evergreen tree is a tree for all seasons, and so are Christians who determine to dress themselves in faith's foliage. Not only in the book of Jeremiah but also in David's psalms the happy person is described as one whose "delight is in the law of the Lord, and on his law he meditates day and night. He is like a tree planted by streams of water, which yields its fruit in season and whose leaf does not wither. Whatever he does prospers" (Psalm 1:2-3).

The more the sap of Scripture fills my branches, the more my leaves shine. The sap must flow unhindered through the branches. It is my job to confess and abandon sin so there will be no blockages hindering the flow of life. This life, given through the Word of God, will produce an ever green tree. "It does not fear when heat comes; its leaves are always green" (Jeremiah 17:8). Read the Bible every day, and obey it every moment. Then your leaves will be ever green.

You Offer Healing

We are a nation that takes more pills than any other nation on earth. But pills will not give me power. Pills will not give me peace. Pills will not freshen my spiritual life. I need spiritual medicine to achieve that. In Revelation 22:1, John saw "the river of the water of life . . . flowing from the throne of God and of the Lamb." John noticed that the leaves of the trees that lined the river's banks were used for "the healing of the nations" (Revelation 22:2). What a beautiful picture. We may borrow the picture and apply it to ourselves, for Scripture uses the same symbol to describe the happy person who is planted by the river of God with her roots in the river of life.

Our lives should offer relief from the heat and shelter from the storm to those who need it. People should take one look at our ever green lives and make a beeline for us. Our lives should be full of healing, relief, and balm.

I think of a friend who always had time for everyone who came her way. I watched her as we worked together with teenagers. She would be walking down a corridor in the big castle, which was the youth center where we lived and worked, and a young person would stop her to ask a question. To me, many of those questions seemed trivial or unnecessary. She would stop and give the young person her total attention, deal with the request, and then carry on toward her goal. She could be interrupted a hundred times and would always exhibit this patient, healing care. There were always plenty of healing leaves on her tree. She is one of the most ever green people I know.

Are your leaves used for healing? You can be a tree of life for others. If I think about my life in recent days and years, I ask myself, "Have people beaten a path to my door because they know where help can be found?" I want to be a tree like Jeremiah describes with its roots in the river, its leaves ever green, and fruit that never fails.

When I heard about my father's cancer, I knew the heat was on. Coming from a family with little evangelical background, I knew there would be lots of opportunities to offer my leaves for healing in the days to come. But this was my great test, too! This was my beloved father who was entering the valley of the shadow. I would be struggling with my own huge sense of loss. How could I help others when I needed such a lot of help myself?

The answer was the river, the river of life. Life in the Spirit offered a source of life to me in the very face of death. My job would be to keep my roots in the river, my leaves full of sap, and stay ever green. It was a hard, hot, desert experience for me, but the Spirit of God was sufficient to supply all I needed, not only for myself, but also for others. God was indeed a life-giving spring.

Another time I found myself confined to the house through illness for a long period of time, and I couldn't get out to church or enjoy fellowship with my Christian friends. I expected to find myself shriveling up spiritually. Instead, I had no alternative but to send out my roots into the stream. I enjoyed such a rich time of renewal and refreshment that I was sorry when I recovered!

When we experienced a tragedy in our family and I wondered if I would ever smile again, I was able to draw the water of life into my branches and make sure my leaves were full of sap. It was no surprise that others in the same circumstances found their way to my tree, where we found healing together.

You Overcome Fear and Worry

One thing is very clear: Those whose roots are in the river get a handle on fear and worry. Jeremiah used the words *fear* and *worry* in his short parable. "It does not *fear* when heat comes" and "It has no *worries* in a year of drought" (Jeremiah 17:8, italics added). Fear and worry are not fruit of the Spirit but rather fruit of the flesh. This is because fear and worry denote a lack of trust and confidence in the Lord.

The longer my roots rest in the river, the better I will deal with fear and worry. It is as simple as that. When I look at the entire life of Jeremiah, I can see that he lived in the heat of life in drought conditions. The heat was on him all the days of his life. There was a drought of leadership in the land, a drought of belief on behalf of the people, a drought of the word of the Lord because most of the prophets spoke lies, and a drought of support in every dimension for Jeremiah himself. There was a drought of friends, of supportive family, of health and wealth. All around him people were worrying about their past, present, and future. God was Jeremiah's past, present, and future!

Jeremiah encouraged himself in the Lord and kept his roots in the river. When he lost faith and confidence in the character and workings of God, he came back to the sap of God's Word and flourished again. When he put his faith into operation, he had no worries or fears. God proved to be bigger than them all.

For years I tried to deal with my many fears one by one. The fear of flying was very real and almost paralyzing to me. I tried to concentrate on overcoming that particular fear. Then I had a fear of speaking in front of "important" people, and a worry about my children not growing up to love the Lord. I feared the hospital and the anesthetic. I feared the absences of my husband when away on missions. I worried about our financial security as missionaries and our loss of benefits when we immigrated to America.

As each worry came along, I concentrated all my efforts on overcoming the worry of the day. Then one day I decided I would stop doing that and concentrate on the main thing. When we do the main thing—making sure our roots are in the river—we develop greater faith in God's ability to help with all and any of our individual worries. This is a huge step forward in dealing with our fears and concerns.

Because of the years of drought I have experienced, the worries of life seem less frightening to me. What God did for me in the past he will do for me in the future. Why should he do anything else? He will not be anything less than he has been. He never changes his mind or his character. I can bank on that.

You Bear Fruit

And what about the fruit? There are many varieties of trees. But the Lord's trees are fruit trees. As if it is not enough to have your roots in the river and your leaves ever green, the trees of the Lord described here have their branches laden with fruit. Life in the Spirit is healing life, green life, and fruitful life. It is the life of the Spirit as described in Galatians 5:22-23: "The fruit of the Spirit is love, joy, peace, patience, kindness, goodness, faithfulness, gentleness and self-control." Paul had already told the Galatians, "The only thing that counts is faith expressing itself through love" (Galatians 5:6). Love is being primarily concerned with others' well-being, regardless of the cost to yourself. Love shows itself in service.

At a Bible conference the guests were asked to help with the chores. They were paying guests, but the school was short on staff. As the guests arrived, they were asked to sign up for a chore to do. The chores ranged from serving at tables to cleaning or vacuuming the rooms to helping in the kitchen. These chores were called "privileges." I was fascinated to watch this play out. We were served with love, care, and big smiles by staff and guests alike. Everyone's leaves shone, and the fruit of the Spirit—love, joy, patience, and kindness—were evident.

A Christian counts service a privilege. It is the fruit of the Spirit! To become a person who lives a life totally focused on God is to become a person who "has no worries in a year of drought and never fails to bear fruit," the fruit of the Spirit (Jeremiah 17:8). This will manifest itself in serving others—even strangers—instead of being served oneself.

When you are bearing the fruit of the Spirit, you will express love in action to a spouse who doesn't "love" you anymore, or a child who doesn't "like" you anymore, or a mother-in-law who doesn't talk to you anymore, or a workmate who doesn't respect you anymore. And all this because your branches are laden with the fruit of the Spirit. You can be patient with the impatient, kind to the cruel, good to the bad, consistent with the unfaithful, gentle to the rough, forgiving to the ones who have hurt you, and able to control your temper when all of those around you have lost theirs.

In John's grand vision of the trees in heaven he notes that these trees are "bearing twelve crops of fruit, yielding its fruit every month" (Revelation 22:2). This is a picture of God's everlasting, constant presence. Has there been a new crop of fresh fruit growing in your life?

You Share Fruit

Do you know anyone who needs a good spiritual meal? a piece of fruit? Is there anyone starved for Scripture because no one has shown her how to connect with the Spirit and produce fruit on her own branches? I do. I meet them all the time. They are folk who remind me of the Ethiopian eunuch. The story in Acts 8:26-39 describes this man from Ethiopia riding along on a desert road reading from the book of Isaiah. At God's direction Philip, like a tree with his roots in the river and his leaves full of sap, ran alongside the carriage and heard the Ethiopian reading. "Do you understand what you are reading?" Philip asked.

The man replied, "How can I unless someone explains it to me?" At which point Philip hopped up into the carriage and explained to the man how to interpret the Scriptures for himself. The eunuch ended up understanding about the river of his redemption and asking to be baptized as a believer in Jesus. Then he continued on his way rejoicing.

My words should feed people's souls because they are God's words that he has explained to me. I can find the "seekers" of this world and offer them the fruit of my life.

I have had the privilege of teaching the Bible for years. But if I can teach others how to teach it, I have doubled my usefulness. I have studied the Bible for years, but if I can teach people to mine its treasures for themselves, I have enriched their lives much more. The fruit of my life should nourish others, particularly by helping them to nourish themselves and then go on to feed others with their discoveries. If my life is to be a life that never fails to bear fruit, it will show patience in affliction, gratitude in prosperity, and zeal as the opportunities arise to offer my life to others.

SO WHERE ARE YOU ROOTED?

Will we ever get over succumbing to the devil's notion that a tree planted by the river should be an object of pity? That a scrub bush has a much better handle on life? The devil wants us to believe he can supply all we need to deal with life itself if we will only bow down and worship him. That's nonsense! Look at the lives of scrub bushes, and pity them, for they have no roots and no river, no leaves when the heat comes, no fruit. What's so beautiful about that?

The simple principles are as follows. First ask yourself, *Do I possess the Spirit?* If not, or if you are unsure, make sure. Pray, "Please, God, will you forgive my sin and invade my life?" Then thank him for answering your prayer. Second, having made sure of his Spirit in your life, ask yourself, *Do I know anything of living in the power of these spiritual truths?* If not, examine your roots. Next, spend time deciding which river you are placing your roots in. Change the situation if need be.

Think about the "sap" of Scripture. Does it fill your branches? What will you do about that if the answer is no? Will you purchase a good study Bible, sign up for a Bible course, buy some teaching tapes, or join a Bible study? Ask God to show you your tree as he sees it.

Is there any fruit on your tree? Are your branches laden with it, or is there a lone orange hanging on a twig? Read Galatians 5:22-23. Pray about this description of the fruit of the Spirit. Finally, as you put out your roots in the direction of the river, let them down into its depths. Be done with dabbling in the shallow streams at Easter and Christmas! Then leave them there, and see what God will grow in your life and show in your life. May Jeremiah's parable be the blessing to you it has been to me.

TIME OUT

These worksheets can be used in groups, in church classes, or with individuals as a discipling tool. They can also be used in a personal quiet time.

Take Time

1. Who is the Holy Spirit? He is the ultimate basis of revelation and the divine agent in our redemption. The Holy Spirit is the executive of the Godhead. He receives equal honor with the Father and the Son. His are all the attributes of deity and eternity. See for yourself. Look up these verses, and name the divine attribute described.

   • Genesis 1:2; Job 33:4
   • Psalm 139:7
   • John 14:26
   • John 15:26
   • Romans 8:26
   • I Corinthians 2:10
   • I Corinthians 12:11
   • I Timothy 4:1
   • Hebrews 9:14

2. Read the parable of the tree and the bush in Jeremiah 17:5-8. Discuss the spiritual implications of this parable. Share any applications to which you can relate. Would you describe yourself as a bush in the wasteland or a tree by the river?
3. Read Galatians 5:22-23. Which aspect of the fruit of the Spirit do you struggle with most?
4. What do you think is the most important principle that releases the power of the Holy Spirit? Repentance? Prayer? Faith?
5. Discuss how the sap of Scripture can flow through your branches. Share ways you can learn the Bible.

Prayer Time

1. Praise God for his Holy Spirit.
2. Praise God for the river of reconciliation that flows from the throne.
3. Pray for people to get their roots in the river.
4. Pray for scrub bushes you know who need transplanting into God.
5. Pray for leaders in the church that they would be faithful, fresh, and fruitful.
6. Pray for yourself and your family.

A Letter to God

Write a letter to God asking him to make your life an ever green tree, laden with fruit.

CHAPTER SEVEN

FAITH TO HANDLE CONFLICT

HIS MAN ON YOUR TEAM

I know, O Lord, that a man's life is not his own;
it is not for man to direct his steps.
JEREMIAH 10:23

WHO HASN'T HAD DIFFICULT PEOPLE IN THEIR LIVES? HOW many of us have come unglued when called to work with someone who drives us crazy? Some people find it really hard to work with people! They would rather fly solo and be their own boss. Perhaps they have a difficult personality, hold strong opinions, can't delegate, or feel they need to do everything themselves. I don't know how Jeremiah and Baruch felt about working with other people, but I do know that God had a partnership in mind for both of them.

God said, "It is not good for the man to be alone" (Genesis 2:18). Adam agreed, so God made Eve—taking her from Adam's prime rib! It seems God likes to see us work in twos. He is all for one man having one woman. Marriage is God's idea. "Two are better than one," says Ecclesiastes 4:9. In marriage as well as ministry, God puts one and one together for his own good reasons and purposes. When it was time for the disciples to set off into ministry, Jesus sent them out two by two (Mark 6:7). Among other things, he has companionship and mutual encouragement in mind. "It is not good for the man [or woman!] to be alone."

In marriage you have a choice about the one with whom you will spend the rest of your life. In ministry, however, other people often choose our partners for us. The church gives us our colleagues. And so often it seems that the church would be a fun place except for the people in it! How often does the women's ministry place two women who can't abide each other together on a committee? How often do the elders call a new member to the staff without checking with the rest of the team? And whether we choose our partners or not, it is in both marriage and ministry that Satan sees his chance to work a whole lot of mischief. He knows if he can't get us from outside the camp, he will get us from inside.

Edinburgh castle in Scotland had never been captured in its history until a traitor let down the drawbridge from within and the enemy ran amok. So it is with us. Satan works with the enemy within us—our old nature—to bring us down. We need to learn not to let the drawbridge down! He knows very well that strong personalities clash. He is the father of dissension.

They say that opposites attract. It was certainly true in Stuart's and my case. My husband is laid back, and I am habitually uptight. He is full of fun whereas I have to enter "Have fun—Thursday" on my schedule, or it doesn't happen! He is very precise where details are concerned while I am a dreamer and love to exaggerate. Opposites do indeed attract, but give the marriage time, and opposites begin to irritate! If this is true in marriage, it is all the more true where strangers are put together in ministry. And if it is true in our time, then it was certainly true in Bible times.

In the New Testament, Paul and Barnabas had their disagreements. They had a falling-out over giving young John Mark another chance after he had let them down on a missionary journey (Acts 15:37-40). And look at Jeremiah and Baruch in the Old Testament. Jeremiah's temperament is legendary, for he has gone down in history as "the weeping prophet." All who knew him said he was a melancholy individual. Whether he started off life this way or not, we don't know. By the time he linked up with Baruch, he had wept his way through not a few laments and was well on his way to earning his reputation of weeping. It could be that life in all its harshness caused the sadness in his soul, or he may have just been made that way.

Our oldest son, David, was not an early talker. When he did utter his first words, however, they were clear and concise: "Oh dear," he sighed! Guess who he had been hanging around—his mother! David's sober side surfaced first, and we discovered that he was certainly influenced by his mother's moans and groans. (I am melancholy too!) His temperament was a truly serious one. God had given him his personality.

Baruch, on the other hand, was named "Blessed." Let us presume the name speaks for his character or personality. God, having a wry sense of humor, put this weeping prophet and blessed scribe together. We could call them "Weepy" and "Happy." God told them: "Just do it, and do it together!" Now that was quite a challenge. There is no doubt that the two men had little in common but the Lord, but that was quite enough to make their partnership work.

MAKE YOUR DIFFERENCES WORK

Face it, difficult people are decidedly different. Even people who love each other are going to have to learn to make their differences work. Stuart and I are partners in both marriage and ministry. Working together to raise a family to love and serve the Lord and working together in mission and the church have tested us. Both marriage and ministry have tested us because we are two very different people. We learn differently, have very different speaking styles, and plan and execute our lives differently. The differences surfaced shortly after the wedding and have continued unabated for forty-four years!

Early on in our married life I well remember Stuart's wonderful way of preparing sermons. It seemed to come so naturally to him. He would wait until near the time he had to speak, concentrate on the subject at hand, and come up with a great talk and relevant illustrations that would hold people spellbound. I, on the other hand, would worry my way through reams of research and notes and start preparing months in advance. I would get in more and more of a muddle. In the end I would give up and use one of Stuart's sermons instead!

Once after my traveling husband had been out of town for

months, he returned to the bosom of his family and began to travel to different towns to speak at the invitation of various churches. As he drove out of the driveway one Sunday, I felt myself going cold all over. The previous week I had been to the particular church he was headed for and had used his very good sermon on Lazarus. *Surely,* I thought in panic, *surely, he wouldn't preach the same sermon! After all, he has hundreds to choose from.*

I had a really miserable day praying hard that the Lord would block the word *Lazarus* completely out of my husband's mind. When he walked into the house that night, I took one look at his face and asked, "Lazarus?"

"Lazarus!" he replied.

"Oh no," I said, smiling and embarrassed.

"Jill," Stuart said, "after I finished my sermon on Lazarus, this woman came barreling up to me and said, 'Ooh, you stole your wife's talk!' "

That day my man sat me down and gave me some help in sermon preparation—something I had never had the opportunity to learn. I learned to develop my own style and study habits according to the way God had fashioned me. Since that fateful day Stuart and I have traveled the world together, learning to make our differences work with greater impact for the kingdom.

Not long ago we arrived at a convention where both of us were speaking. When I opened the program, I realized that the organizers had made a mistake. Both Stuart and I were slated to speak on the same subject—Lazarus!

"Oh no!" I gasped. "One of us will have to change our topic."

"Why?" inquired my patient husband.

"Because we can't both speak on the same passage of Scripture," I replied, stating what I thought was the obvious.

"Jill," replied Stuart, "they'll never know!"

And they never did know! Our styles and delivery have developed over the years to such a degree that we can even take the same passage of Scripture and have it come out of our personalities uniquely different.

Someone has said that preaching is really "the proclamation of truth through personality." When Stuart with his happy nature preached on Lazarus that day, his text was "Lazarus, come forth!" Mine was (you guessed it), "Jesus wept." This was just a "Happy" and a "Weepy" happily at work!

There is no doubt in my mind that Jeremiah and Baruch had not only vastly different temperaments but also different styles of writing and speaking. At one point Baruch read the message from a manuscript while Jeremiah spoke freely and powerfully without notes, often using dramatic means to illustrate his talks.

Baruch had to record the words of the prophet. Some think that Baruch recorded some of the messages that God gave to Jeremiah in his own gifted style while he relayed others word for word. How did these two men put their differences to work for the good of the kingdom and the honor of God's name? It could not have been easy, but it was done, and done well, and to God's glory!

Are you a Happy or a Weepy? Does your personality match Baruch's or Jeremiah's? Has God locked you up in marriage or ministry with someone the exact opposite of you? How are you rising to the challenge? Are you giving God a chance to accomplish what he had in mind when he yoked you together, or are you letting down the drawbridge to the devil? You have to find a way to make your differences work for you and not against you.

LET GOD CHOOSE YOUR TEAM

You will be able to deal more effectively with a difficult person if you believe that *God* has put the other person in your marriage or on your team. We are not to mess with the call of God in someone else's life. He has chosen this sometimes irritating counterpart not to annoy you or make your job more difficult but rather to match personalities up to enhance the overall outcome of his purposes. I am not free to pray as the little boy prayed, "Please God, send Derek Smith to another camp next year!"

Not only has he put "Derek Smith" in my life, he may have put him there deliberately because he has something very special for

Derek Smith to do for him and for me! God made this person just like he or she is, and he didn't consult me! I am not talking about things that need to be addressed in another's life that have nothing to do with personality. People need to face up to their sin and bad habits and confront them. But we should do the same with our own bad attitudes.

An assistant pastor's wife wrote and told me, "I can hardly talk to the senior pastor's wife. I think she hates me. We're so different. It's not just a generational thing."

What a sad letter! But I would have to tell you this is not at all uncommon. The fact that it is not uncommon, however, does not mean the situation should be allowed to go from bad to worse. Someone—like you or me!—should try to intervene. The problem is, people can be so annoyed with their opposite that they decide the best thing to do is to opt out and start over with someone new. *Perhaps if I found another person more like me, I would be better off,* they think. But God is not into "cloning." He is into counterparting!

BE WILLING TO PLAY SECOND FIDDLE

Another step to maturity in dealing with difficult people is being willing to defer, to play "second fiddle." You should not only be able to defer to people when you are weaker than they are in some areas but also when you are as strong as or stronger than they are in some areas! Perhaps you have a leader of a team who is weak, yet she has been put in leadership and you have not. I have learned that is not my business; it is God's.

Years ago I read a quote that has served me well ever since: "It matters more than tongue can tell, to play the second fiddle well." This is especially true when you have first-fiddle gifts. Angie Mills, a colleague of mine at the youth center where we worked, had first-fiddle gifts, but she unselfishly played second fiddle to me for ten years. Eventually she took over the work. Baruch undoubtedly had first-fiddle abilities, yet he deferred to the younger man and served him instead of launching out on his own, writing his own best-seller, and furthering his own career. It takes a big man to do little things for a time, but that is often the way of the cross and, incidentally, of the crown.

There was a time when I watched my husband in this situation. We were serving a youth mission. Stuart had been asked to go on staff as treasurer of the organization because of his training and expertise in banking. How this would work out we had no idea. My husband already had been preaching all over the country as a layperson, but the youth mission did not know the extent of his giftedness in this area.

Each week we had conferences where there would be an invited speaker. Most were excellent, a few were good, and one or two were mediocre (in my less-than-humble opinion). It began to be really hard for me to sit through the good and the mediocre ones as I thought of my husband's gifts and believed he could do a better job! Why was he passing out hymnbooks at the back of the auditorium instead of occupying the pulpit? How could we have gotten ourselves into a situation where he was asked to play second fiddle when he had first-fiddle gifts?

I began to complain to the Lord about this, and then I began to complain to Stuart as well. "Jill, you're not helping me," my husband replied. "Will it matter in a hundred years who passed out the hymnbooks and who passed out the Word? We are on a team. Remember, God brought us here, and here we stay until God leads us out as surely as God led us in!" I struggled on, feeling more and more frustrated. It was one thing to learn to be a weak link on a strong chain, but it was far harder to learn to be a strong link on a weak chain!

Then one day the leader of our work invited Stuart to take the Sunday service—and that was it! From then on Stuart preached regularly. Eventually we found doors opening to us through that same leader all over the world. Thinking about it now, I realize that "no plan of [God's] can be thwarted" as Job put it (Job 42:2). If we will follow God's directions and be obedient, he will work out the details. Baruch could have written his own book, but would his work have been preserved in the millions of Bibles across the centuries? I think not! God works in a mysterious way his wonders to perform!

It is also difficult to work with a lot of talent on your team but little equipment. When you have very few fiddles, or only a bow without a fiddle, it is frustrating to compromise the work you are doing. It boils down to sometimes being willing to work below your capacity.

In his business career Stuart was a bank inspector. In missions he was treasurer of the fellowship. After handling high finance in the largest British bank, he handled "low" finance in the mission. Often missions organizations do not have the money for state-of-the-art equipment or even for trained staff. The annoying situations that can arise when you are working below your ability or training—with a staff that is not always up to par and with equipment that is out-of-date or nonexistent—are grounds for an explosion of tension. On the other hand, they can also be grounds for the production of the fruit of the Spirit in your life. I am quite sure that Jeremiah and his amanuensis had very poor working conditions. This must have stimulated creativity and originality!

I loved a poster I saw on the mission field over a secretary's desk in an office in Nigeria. The work environment left an awful lot to be desired. It read:

> *We the unwilling,*
> *Led by the unknowing,*
> *Are doing the impossible*
> *For the ungrateful.*
> *We have done so much*
> *For so long with so little,*
> *We are now qualified*
> *To do anything with nothing!*

When you think about it, Jesus worked below his capacity in Nazareth for thirty years! When he began his "ministry," his staff did not include the best-trained operatives in the world. But Jesus was willing to work with potential in people instead of the finished product, and do it for God—and for us. That is the key!

CULTIVATE A SERVANT SPIRIT

A lot of people in the church are only interested in serving in an advisory capacity! Serving God and serving others as we serve God is what God desires. It may be that God has a leadership role in mind for you, and it may not be. What we all need to cultivate is a servant spirit that mirrors the Master's heart.

I have learned to start with my language. I try to listen to myself talking and watch my mouth at all times. I have learned to ask a committee that invites me to speak to them, "How can I serve you?" instead of "What can I teach you?" I have a sentence written in the flyleaf of my Bible that says, "Let another praise you and not your own lips." And I try to await the invitation to "come up higher" instead of hiking up the hill of importance myself.

Jenny, the girl who led me to Christ, told me to wake up every morning and go out into a new day looking for people to bless. I didn't know what she meant as I had been somewhat of a curse before my conversion! "How do you 'be a blessing' instead of a curse?" I asked her.

"Just go out into each day, and every time you meet someone ask, 'What can I do for you?' " she answered.

Now this was pretty radical for me as I was used to asking people, "What can you do for me?" not "What can I do for you?" But I found out that it worked! And that was the way I learned to be a blessing and cultivate a servant spirit.

One of the first times I asked that question was in a church I joined when I was a student teacher. There was a sad-looking girl sitting in the pew in front of me. One day I introduced myself to her, and after talking to her for a bit, I asked "the question."

"What can I do for you?" I inquired with a bright but somewhat false smile.

Immediately she brightened up and said, "Oh, do you really mean you want to do something for me?"

"Yes," I answered, feeling a bit apprehensive at her eager response.

"Well," she said, "I am my mother's caregiver. She is an invalid, and though I care for her, I have to work as well. Could you come and do some housecleaning for us? I never have time to do any of the extra things that need doing around the house."

My heart sank. I had never liked housecleaning. I didn't want to do my own, never mind hers! I had expected her to say, "Will you come and read the Bible to my mother and tell her about the Lord?" That would have been fine, but not *this!*

She didn't seem to notice my apprehension as by now she was so excited and saying, "Tomorrow? I'll tell you how to get there, and I'll leave you a list." And she was gone.

The next day I apprehensively approached the house. What would she ask me to do? I had thought a lot about the list she had promised me, and I wasn't at all sure I wanted to go inside and read it. The list was long, the lady was not particularly appreciative of my efforts, and I left feeling decidedly dejected. I determined to have a word with Jenny as soon as possible and tell her what I thought about her great idea of asking "the question." I also decided to stay out of the girl's way in church.

Jenny merely laughed when I told her the story, remarking that God would use the effort even if my spirit had been less than sweet! Sure enough, the girl found me again, happily gave me another list, and said she would expect me every Tuesday from then on!

Struggling with the whole thing, I turned up the next Tuesday, and then the next and the next. One day, long after I had given up expecting it, someone thanked me. It was the old lady's brother. "Why should a young lady like you make yourself a servant to strangers?" he asked me.

I told him, "Because I am a Christian and Jesus said we should be servants of all." I must admit I felt like a huge hypocrite. But from then on, all sorts of relatives appeared when I was working through my list, and the Lord began a ministry through me that spilled out beyond the walls of the old lady's room.

Then I understood that what was happening *in* me as the Spirit of God began creating a servant spirit was just as important as what was happening *through* me—the witnessing to the family. He was making me like him. It was a little time before I dared ask "the question" again! But through the years I have never been out of work for the Lord by using that very simple question.

At some point Baruch asked Jeremiah, "What can I do for you?" Jeremiah gave him a list! I am sure there were household chores on Baruch's list, too! Baruch manifested a servant spirit in doing the things on Jeremiah's list and, in so doing, became more like the God he served.

We need to realize that we serve Christ when we serve people. Mother Teresa taught her Sisters of Mercy to see the face of Christ in the destitute people they served. Jesus said, "Whatever you did for one of the least of these brothers of mine, you did for me" (Matthew 25:40).

Volunteer. Sign up. Respond to a notice in the church bulletin or a need in the community. Give your life away. Ask "the question." Start with your own time and not your children's time or your husband's time. At some point Baruch volunteered. He put his first fiddle on the shelf and said to Jeremiah, "What can I do for you?"

Jeremiah told him, "Be my helper. Take second place and work for me."

When Baruch did, he was well on the way to mirroring the Master's heart.

THANK GOD FOR THOSE DIFFICULT PEOPLE

I thank God for the difficult people in my life, for I have discovered that they are not always difficult. Many times as I have gotten to know them, they have proved to be different and not difficult. I thank God for their grace in putting up with me! As I am driven to pray about personality conflicts, I hear the Lord reminding me that he has deliberately brought his children into my orbit for good reasons. Sometimes he will tell me those reasons, and sometimes he won't. He nudges me by his Spirit to look for ways to elevate others—difficult others or different others, people who choose to do and say things in a very different way from the way I would do or say them. I talk sternly to myself and tell myself, "This is really none of my business. This is God's business, and I can rest assured that he knows exactly what he is doing."

Chip, chip, chip goes the chisel. Most times I can say, "Chip away, Lord. Make me like you."

STEPS TO HANDLING CONFLICT

When we first came to the States, a lady called us one day to tell us she was suing her husband for divorce. They were both members of our church.

"What's the trouble?" I heard my husband ask her.

"We're incompatible," she explained.

"That's the reason for marriage, not divorce," my husband replied cheerfully. "Why don't you come in and see us?" They came in and are still together today. They are also busy in the church and about the Lord's business.

Personality conflicts and temperamental differences are fertile grounds for difficulties and discouragements in marriage and ministry. But they are also great opportunities to put the power of God to work and show the world how Christians can love each other and work together against all odds—even when people are very different. The relationship of the prophet Jeremiah and his scribe, Baruch, shows us how.

How do we get along with people? One of the greatest things we may have going for us is the choice we have to look at people as God looks at them. No matter how they irritate us, we can choose to love them when we don't like them and work with them when no one else will. Both Jeremiah and Baruch chose to let the chisel of difficult people make them more like God. After all, God has to deal with difficult people all the time. He is practiced at it and is more than willing to share his secrets with us.

Find the Common Ground

The first thing to do is find common ground. As far as Jeremiah was concerned, the common ground was their common calling. He knew that God had called Baruch to his task as surely as he had called Jeremiah to his. He was equally sure that the talented scribe had been gifted by the Spirit in order to fulfill the work that God had put in his hands. He believed that Baruch had been commissioned, not by him but by the Lord Almighty, to get the message out. In short, Jeremiah believed that God's man was on his team.

But it has to work both ways—it takes two. Did Baruch believe these same lofty things about his brother Jeremiah? We shall see that he had his doubts about the whole venture and about his partnership with Jeremiah in particular. But at the end of the day, the two men could look back on a forty-year-plus partnership in the Lord's work. They had done it, and they had done it with grace and style.

One of the things that has helped me down through the years has been to look at the Baruchs in my life (I'm "Weepy," remember) and believe that God has picked them. And those whom God has picked must not be "unpicked"! I am not to mess with someone else's calling. When I find nothing in common but our primary call to discipleship, I know that's enough common ground on which to build. In other words, what we have in common helps us with what we don't! To have spiritual respect for one another goes a long way in overcoming personality.

Our commonality in our calling focuses our eyes on the Lord and takes our eyes off each other. Once when I was having a little trouble with a fellow worker with whom I had nothing in common, I kept saying to myself, *But we are both for the Lord, and for the sheep.* This was our heart, what we both wanted. This is what made our team of two disparate people work. So start by finding the common ground.

You have both been forgiven by the same and only Savior of the world. You have both received the Holy Spirit. You are both gifted by God for your secondary callings. You are both concerned that God's plans not be hindered. You both love Jesus. You both care about people. You are both intent on facing God at the end of the day with nothing to be ashamed about. You both believe the Bible. You both believe in the deity of Christ and the church of which Christ is the head. You both love to engage in worship, and while your styles of worship may differ, you both agree that God should be worshiped in spirit and in truth. See what a lot of things you have in common!

So work at finding common ground. Make a list if it helps you. If you make a list of the things you have in common, you can take that list with you into God's throne room and spend some time praising God for all the ways you think alike.

Celebrate the Differences

Next, celebrate the differences. Remember that differences don't necessarily mean that the person is difficult. If you are a "Weepy," try laughing at one of "Happy's" jokes. Go on, it won't kill you! Even if you don't think it's very funny. And if you are "Happy," try enjoying one of "Weepy's" laments. I am sure both Jeremiah and Baruch learned to enjoy another mood! Learn to be positive or learn to be sorrowful, as the case may be!

A lady asked me, "What can I do to get my joy back?" She was panicked. Our secular society and even our Christian society often give the impression that we *have* to be happy no matter what is happening in our lives.

"Why don't you just enjoy another mood?" I suggested to the lady.

She was aghast. "Surely God wants me to be happy all the time," she said hopefully.

"Do you like music?" I asked her.

"Yes," she responded.

"Are all the songs you like in major key?" I asked next.

"No, of course not!" she answered.

"Isn't a song in minor key just as pretty as one in major key?" I inquired.

She nodded.

"It is all right to be in a somber mood sometimes," I assured her.

In the same way, it's all right to major on majors sometimes. Paul says: "Whatever is true, whatever is noble, whatever is right, whatever is pure, whatever is lovely, whatever is admirable—if anything is excellent or praiseworthy—think about such things" (Philippians 4:8). It will do Weepy a world of good to have a positive companion to point out the pluses of the situation. As the rhyme says, "Two men looked through prison bars; one saw mud, and the other saw stars." Jeremiah had reason to look at a lot of mud in his life. He also could take the opportunity to look up at such times and see the stars. I know God used Baruch to help his friend do some stargazing.

Once when I was just about to be released from the hospital, the doctor found a hernia that had been caused by an appendix operation. "This will mean you have to stay and get this seen to, I'm afraid," he told me.

As I was readmitted to the hospital on the spot, I was tempted to descend into depression. God sent one of my friends to visit me that afternoon. She was not the sort of hospital visitor I wanted that day, as she was Happy personified. "Oh, how wonderful, Jill," she gushed when I mournfully told her what had happened. "God must have all sorts of people here he wants you to tell about the Lord!"

I didn't want to tell anyone about the Lord at the time, I only wanted to go home! *Anyway, it's all right for her,* I thought bitterly. *She isn't the one being readmitted to the hospital!* However, I thought about her cheerful words, and when Sunday rolled around, I asked the nurse in charge if I could hold a little church service from my wheelchair. To my amazement, she was quite enthusiastic. She not only organized the church service but also wheeled various and sundry other people in wheelchairs into the ward to join in! *Thank God for my friend, Happy,* I thought, as I happily told them all about the Lord. What would I have done without her? I have no doubt that Baruch played a similar role in Jeremiah's life, encouraging him to use his troubles as a pulpit from which to preach God's Word.

Celebrating the differences means being determined to appreciate the ways people are different. If you concentrate on one major difference at a time and work on making a real mental effort to find something you can appreciate about it, you will succeed. When you have found a major difference, think about it in a determinedly positive way. Next, pray about it, and thank God for your partner and the major difference you have found.

Because Stuart and I are so very different, we have had the opportunity to do a lot of this sort of thing. When we first came to the States in 1970, people began to ask us to speak together. Often they would ask us to speak about marriage. I was so excited. Up to this point, we had both been busy speaking, but on different sides of the Atlantic! Now we could put our gifts together for the Lord.

I remember our first joint speaking engagement. It was in Chicago, and it was a marriage retreat. True to form, I began to prepare at least three months in advance. "What shall we speak about?" I asked my husband happily.

"Jill, it's three months away. We'll talk about it the week before," answered my husband.

I was horrified. I could never be properly prepared a week before an event. "Well, at least let's choose the passage of Scripture so I can be thinking about it," I suggested.

"Jill, I have a church to run," replied my husband. "We don't need to start on this yet. We have dozens of meetings before this one."

I tried not to bug him about it but did anyway, to no avail! The week before came, and I was panicked. "Do you *yet* know what we are doing?" I asked him in an accusing voice.

"Not yet, Jill," he replied unconcerned. "I have a funeral and a deacon's meeting to go to before I'll have time to pull it together." The day arrived, and we had only a vague idea of what we would do. "Don't worry about it," my husband kept saying. "You'll see, all sorts of things will come to mind just when you need them to!"

All sorts of things were coming to mind, but not the sort of things that should have been! Getting into the car with a strained silence between us, I promptly burst into tears and wept copiously all the way to Chicago! "Whatever shall we do?" I sobbed as we arrived at the venue.

"Why don't we both get up there and analyze what went wrong?"

suggested Stuart cheerfully. "Then we can talk it out in front of the people and explain how we resolve a conflict in our marriage!"

It was too late to do anything else. To my absolute amazement, I found myself up on the platform talking the whole thing over in front of a few hundred interested people!

Stuart began by explaining that we had had a difference of opinion on the way to the meeting and they were very welcome to listen in as we resolved it! And so we talked it out as we usually solved our disputes. We discussed how very opposite we are, how our way of doing things is so drastically different, and how it causes problems all the time. Then I apologized for my attitude, and Stuart apologized for his. Next, Stuart said what he appreciated about my way of diligent preparation, and I told him how I admired his wonderful ability to pull things together so quickly. We celebrated each other's differences verbally.

Then we forgot all about the three hundred interested onlookers and told each other how we would begin to make allowances for the other and show consideration for the way each of us worked. We thought up some compromises both of us could make and promised to make them. We smiled at each other, laughed a bit, gave each other a hug, and then suddenly we remembered we had an audience! So Stuart opened his Bible and did what he does best—teach. He spoke on Ephesians 5:21-33, the classic text about how husbands and wives should treat each other. I listened carefully and thought of illustrations from our own marriage that I could use when he had finished. The day flew by. It was wonderful!

That incident happened at least twenty-five years ago, but just this month a man said to me, "Do you remember coming to Chicago to talk about marriage? You came on stage and looked as though you had been crying for a week!" He had been there! "I have never forgotten that," he said.

I bet he hadn't! Neither have I because that was the day Stuart and I began to work on "celebrating the differences" and using those differences as weapons—not against each other, but for God and his kingdom.

Did Baruch, the meticulous scribe, and Jeremiah, the mystical dreamer, ever struggle with putting it all together? You can be certain that they did. They would have had to find their common ground, compromise where necessary, and celebrate their differences.

Understand the Why

Perhaps the differences you are struggling with as you work with the Baruchs or Jeremiahs of your life are not personality differences at all but rather plain obnoxious behavior! Maybe your fellow teammate thinks he or she has a musical gift and insists on singing off-key around you. Perhaps you graduated with honors in flügelhorn!

Maybe your roommate has terrible table manners or a bad habit that drives you crazy. It could be that your fellow leader has a harsh manner when dealing with subordinates and you are forever picking up the pieces of hurt hearts and wounded feelings. Try to step back and ask the "Why?" question. "Why is this person behaving like this?"

When you think of the close quarters that the two servants of the Lord lived in for decades, there must have been many instances of their rubbing each other the wrong way. After all, Baruch was brought up in king's palaces while Jeremiah came from the country. Baruch had the advantage of schooling that fitted him for scribal work and brought him great renown; Jeremiah appears to have been self-taught, full of raw talent and brilliant flashes of inspiration. The partnership reminds me of the film *Amadeus.* Mozart composed with genius, while Salieri, the king's musician, studied at the best music schools and was very talented. But compared to the brilliance of Mozart, Salieri appeared very ordinary.

Try and understand the *why* of people's behavior, and it should help you to tolerate much of it. For example, when Jeremiah's melancholy and depressive spirit brought a pall over the work, Baruch could have helped himself to react properly by trying to imagine what he would have felt like if his feet had been put in the stocks and he had been the one subjected to ridicule and torment all day long. And maybe Jeremiah found a little sympathy for Baruch when he had a hard time toughing it out on occasions. It may be that Jeremiah thought about his friend's background and what he had given up to serve him. In the end, God knows exactly which people he will use as his chisel in our lives to achieve his divine ends.

When I came to Christ, I was in Addenbrook's hospital in Cambridge, England. There was a nurse at that hospital who seemed to be universally hated. Her reputation preceded her when she appeared on our ward four days after I arrived. She was impatient and sarcastic. My fellow patients and I felt she would easily win the "bad nurse of the year" award.

Jenny, the girl next to me, was in considerable pain and running a fever. The difficult nurse arrived at her bedside and said, "You asked for a hot water bottle. Well, here it is!" She then deposited an extremely hot rubber bottle in my friend's bed.

"No, thank you," Jenny whispered, "I'm so hot." But her protests were ignored, and the hot water bottle stayed. I was furious and remonstrated with the nurse but was rudely told to mind my own business. That was the beginning of a running battle with this woman.

After I left the hospital and was back at school, I heard, to my dismay, that the obnoxious nurse had been converted! I couldn't believe it and was, in fact, quite annoyed about it. Now I would have to put up with her turning up at the meetings I went to. I felt like Jonah being mad that the Ninevites had repented! In the days ahead, my worst fears were realized as, sure enough, there she was as large as life! *Well,* I thought to myself, *I needn't be too worried as there are lots of churches in Cambridge, and we could go to different ones.* But there she was one Sunday, in *my* church, in the pew in front of me.

There was a student convention at Keswick in the English Lake District that I signed up for, and to my great annoyance, there was her name on the list. *Well, never mind,* I told myself, *there are lots of buses going to the convention. She could go on one, and I could go on another.* But, you guessed it, when I got on one of the many buses, there she was in the front seat, of course!

Arriving at Keswick, I thought desperately of the myriad bed-and-breakfasts we would all be staying at. *Surely, surely . . .* but yes, she surely was signed up for mine! Wearily getting my room key at the hotel desk, I climbed the quaint little winding stairway figuring out how I could go to breakfast early and avoid her. Opening my door, I burst into the room, and there was my enemy sitting on the one bed! There was dead silence as we looked at each other. Then we both burst out laughing. "Only God would do something like this," she said.

"Only God," I replied.

It took a week at that convention to talk things out, starting with that first long night when we told each other what we both disliked so much about the other. But during that glorious week, we came together as friends and fellow servants of the Jesus we had both come to know and love so recently. We majored on what we had in common, which was precious little, but enough. We both loved Jesus to distraction and shared a common call to give our lives away for him.

We began to appreciate the differences in our personalities, and we both began to understand the *why* of behavior patterns in each other that had driven us both crazy. She came from pain, while I came from plenty. She brought herself up, while I had loving parents. She had been abused, while I had been pampered and spoiled.

God did his work in both of us, and we both heard clearly the *chip, chip, chip* of the chisel. The motto of the Keswick Convention came to have new meaning for me: All One in Christ Jesus.

Maureen and I returned to Cambridge together. Unbelievably, we were friends. Only God can do such things with such disparate people. She went to the mission field, and I supported her. She has prayed for me, and I have prayed for her. We are sisters in kingdom work today—we who are Baruch and Jeremiah.

Realize That You May Be Difficult Too!
Another day when I was having a really hard time with a difficult person in my life and on my team, it dawned on me that maybe she thought I was difficult too! This was a novel thought for me and

quite a shock. That day I read, "In humility consider others better than yourselves" (Philippians 2:3). As I began to actively look for ways that this was true—that she was better than I in different areas of her life—I began to realize how my shortcomings must irritate her. It was a short step from that thought to appreciation of her strengths, which I verbalized to her. I found myself willing to play second fiddle to her first fiddle in those areas where she was strong.

Above all, remember that difficult people are often God's chisel in his hand. He is intent on chiseling the "David" out of us.

> *Chiseled by the people that you bring into my life*
> *People who are difficult and cause me grief and strife.*
> *Teach me, Lord, to honor them and help me, Lord, to see*
> *They're not as near as awkward or as difficult as me.*

TIME OUT

These worksheets can be used in groups, in church classes, or with individuals as a discipling tool. They can also be used in a personal quiet time.

Take Time

1. Define your own personality. Are you more of a Weepy or a Happy? Discuss ways you have made differences in personalities work for you.

2. Think of an "opposite person" in your life. Think of three things you have in common. Write them down. Spend a few moments praying about those things you have in common.

3. Consider that "opposite person" again. Think of three things you don't have in common. Think of some of the positives on that list. Spend a few moments thanking God for those differences.

4. Write a sentence about one of your own traits that you know irritates other people. Pray about it.

5. Reread the poem on page 127. Is the situation on the mission field any different from our own? How?

6. Read I Corinthians 13:2-4. How can playing second fiddle produce this sort of character in us?

7. Read what Jesus said in the following verses about a servant spirit. Make a list of his imperatives from these verses. Then discuss practical ways of cultivating such an attitude.

   - Matthew 4:10
   - Matthew 20:26
   - Matthew 25:21
   - Luke 16:13
   - Luke 17:10
   - John 15:15

8. Read what others said:

- I Corinthians 12:5
- Ephesians 6:7
- Colossians 3:23-24
- 2 Timothy 2:4
- 2 Timothy 2:24

Prayer Time

1. Pray for people in the church and in missions who are locked into difficult situations with difficult people.
2. Pray for difficult people in your own family.
3. Pray for patience, respect, and love.
4. Pray about one thing the Lord has impressed on your heart from this chapter.
5. Pray that God will help you cultivate a servant spirit.

A Letter to God

Write a promise to God in the form of a letter. Post it in prayer.

CHAPTER EIGHT

FAITH WHEN YOU SUFFER

———— ❦ ————

HIS TEARS ON YOUR FACE

Should you then seek great things for yourself?
Seek them not.
JEREMIAH 45:5

IT IS DIFFICULT TO BEAR PRIVATE PAIN PUBLICLY. SOME PEO-
ple share their pain while others find that very difficult. Baruch was
apparently one of those who found it very difficult to share his pain
with others. His inner struggles were just that—*inner* struggles.
They had to do with broken dreams, private pain, the loss of his expectations and ambitions. Some of us can more readily identify with
Baruch than with Jeremiah in this regard. While the prophet wore
his heart on his sleeve, his scribe wrapped his pain in silence and bat-
tled away internally.

Baruch had stood up to be counted for God by siding with Jeremiah and was perhaps surprised at the consequences. If he and Jeremiah were right, then why were they so alone in their stand? True,
they had a few supporters—and some of them among people of
influence in high places—but the backlash from the leadership of
the nation and their own families must have been totally unexpected.

Baruch's heart had drawn him to an unexpected calling, despite
his pedigree. He was the grandson of Mahseiah (Jeremiah 32:12),
who had been the governor of Jerusalem during Josiah's reign
(2 Chronicles 34:8). His brother was the chief chamberlain in the
court of Zedekiah.

With such a background Baruch may have harbored hopes of

high office or of receiving gifts of prophecy, but such dreams were not to be realized.

LAYING DOWN YOUR DREAMS

What do you do when your fondest dreams have to be laid down? When you discover that you will never realize those dreams? When, in fact, your dreams turn into nightmares? When God begins to make it plain that you are to spend your life playing on that second fiddle, functioning in a supporting role? Well, if you are like Baruch, you might get a little depressed! Hidden conflict takes its toll. But Baruch's struggles were, he thought, well hidden from the world and from his partner. We may learn to hide conflict from those closest to us, but we can't hide it from God—as Baruch was to find out.

There is no doubt that the scribe's noble family was unimpressed by the decisions he had made. We all know that family pressure can be the strongest cause for discouragement. Many a family has tried to discourage a child from, as they see it, "throwing his life away" in missions or ministry. To go into a life's work that promises to bring little worldly remuneration seems such a waste to those who see things from a worldly point of view. When parents have spent lots of money on a child's education and given him or her privileges and status, it seems uncalled for that the child would "throw it all away." Apparently Baruch did not have to put up with the dangerous antagonism that Jeremiah faced from his family, but he had enough family pressure to add to his misery.

Jeremiah's relatives and "friends" in Anathoth had warned him, "Do not prophesy in the name of the Lord or you will die by our hands" (Jeremiah 11:21). How incredibly painful this must have been to Jeremiah! He dealt with his private pain by sharing it with his scribe, who wrote down his personal laments. Baruch also recorded God's reply to him:

> If you have raced with men on foot and they have worn you out, how can you compete with horses? If you stumble in

safe country, how will you manage in the thickets by the
Jordan? Your brothers, your own family—even they have
betrayed you; they have raised a loud cry against you.
Do not trust them, though they speak well of you.
(Jeremiah 12:5-6)

It was time to play with the big boys. God knew there was trouble enough ahead for Jeremiah, and he encouraged his servant to
toughen up and face the battle.

Sometimes this is just the message we need, a "toughen up" message. Even though God was concerned about Jeremiah's pain, God
did not allow his servant to wallow in it. "That's how it is, Jeremiah," he told him. "Sometimes following me carries with it a
cost—a cost that hurts—but in the end a cost that is eminently
worth it." God helped Jeremiah to realize he couldn't turn to his
own family for help, as they were part of the problem. Now that
hurt, badly. However, God challenged him to greater faith in the trials that lay ahead.

USING YOUR SORROWS

The beautiful Bayeaux Tapestry has a picture of a bishop accompa-
nying his soldiers into battle. A frightened soldier is pictured running away from the fray toward the safety of the bishop's tent.
However, the tapestry shows the bishop using the sharp end of his
staff to poke and prod the soldier back where he belongs! Underneath, the caption reads, "The bishop encourages his soldier."

Has God ever "encouraged" you like that? I must admit that, like
a frightened sheep, I have oftentimes run away from the hard things
in life and experienced the unmistakable prodding of my heavenly
Shepherd's crook in my little woolly rump! This is how he "encourages" me back into the midst of the battle to do my part.

There was a time when I was afraid of getting up in front of
Christians to speak. God spoke to me about that. In the words he
spoke to Jeremiah he said to me, "If you have raced with men on
foot and they have worn you out, how can you compete with horses?

If you stumble in safe country, how will you manage in the thickets by the Jordan?" (Jeremiah 12:5). I was in safe country. I was learning to race with men on foot. If I could not get up in front of people where it was safe—in a church setting where all my friends were—how would I fare outside the safe confines of the church in evangelistic outreach? In other words, how was I going to be able to get up and give my message in the open-air meetings the church planned to have in the community? I felt the prod of my "bishop's staff" that day and decided I needed to toughen up.

When it was Baruch's time to face the bishop of his soul and feel the prodding of his staff, he had already recorded the Lord's message to Jeremiah about his family. Perhaps Baruch knew, from God's words to Jeremiah, that it would be no good complaining to God about his own troubles. If God had told the prophet to toughen up, what would he say to him? Perhaps it was at this point that Baruch chose to keep his fears to himself and battle on in silence.

He had also witnessed the people's reactions to his friend's message; they had threatened to kill him for preaching it! He had stood by as the leaders of Israel, among whom were his own friends and relatives, reacted violently to the word from the Lord. It was this incident that thoroughly frightened Baruch. After Jeremiah had delivered his significant sermon in the temple with his assistant by his side (Jeremiah 26), Baruch was horrified to witness what happened next. "As soon as Jeremiah finished telling all the people everything the Lord had commanded him to say, the priests, the prophets and all the people seized him and said, 'You must die!'" (Jeremiah 26:8). It took some of the elders who were listening and Ahikam, who supported Jeremiah, to make sure that cooler heads prevailed (Jeremiah 26:24).

Chapter 45 follows this incident chronologically in the Bible, and so we can be pretty sure Baruch was shaken to the core by the proceedings. He realized that taking Jeremiah's side could well cost him his life. But Baruch was convinced that Jeremiah was God's man for the moment. He had wanted to be in the center of God's will, to be where the action was, but suddenly all that changed. So Baruch decided to deal with his discouragement and change of heart in his own way.

His belief in God's message through Jeremiah had not changed. In fact, this was part of the problem. Baruch believed with all his heart that unless the people returned to the Lord, nothing would stop Nebuchadnezzar from taking the city. But this was *his* city, led by *his* relatives. His own family lived here. The terrible judgments he had been recording had to do with the people he loved. To believe this was to experience a pain so intense that it brought forth a heart cry very much like the weeping prophet's. Baruch grieved over what he had to record about Israel's sin and its consequence. His sorrow, pain, and groaning wore him out. His emotional involvement in what he wrote gave him no respite.

So here we have an amazing change. "Happy" has become "Weepy"! "Woe to me! The Lord has added sorrow to my pain; I am worn out with groaning and find no rest," he wails (Jeremiah 45:3). The New Living Translation renders this verse: "I am overwhelmed with trouble! Haven't I had enough pain already? And now the Lord has added more! I am weary of my own sighing and can find no rest." But he wails silently, where no one can hear him—or so he thinks.

First, he grieved about his own life and then about his fears for his loved ones' safety. Now that's a lot of pain! Fast on the heels of the death of his own dreams and ambitions came very real mourning for the deaths of his relatives. That's a lot of loss to handle within a short amount of time. It's certainly enough to give anyone a good dose of faith distress and spiritual depression!

Can you identify with Baruch? Does it seem you have had one thing after another until you are "overwhelmed with sorrow"? Has God added sorrow to your pain? How are you handling it all? Are you, like Jeremiah, letting it all hang out? Or are you, like Baruch, internalizing everything until you are torn up on the inside even though you put on a brave face on the outside?

One way is not better than the other. The important thing is not *how* you handle differences and losses but *that* you handle them! God is concerned about you on the *inside* and the *outside* and is determined to speak to your pain and help you with it.

I think Baruch's greatest pain was wrestling with his doubts about

God. He didn't pray; he couldn't. Why pray to a God who didn't care about what was happening to him? So he indulged in a "pity party" all on his own. Baruch was suffering his own severe case of faith distress. He thought that God was callous and uncaring about his predicament. He had gotten God and life mixed up, just as Jeremiah did. At this point he reminds me of Elijah in the book of Kings, who came to a similarly low point in his life and ministry and ended up saying, "I have had enough, Lord" (1 Kings 19:4). Elijah laid down under a broom tree and wanted to die.

It is an encouragement to me to meet the great men and women of the Bible who had moments like these. Through their experiences God is seen to be a compassionate God who comes to us in our deepest despondency and says, as he said to Elijah, "Get up and eat, for the journey is too much for you" (1 Kings 19:7). He doesn't mollycoddle us but gives us a strong poke with his staff and sends us back into the fray. We will see that God would meet Baruch under his particular broom tree and minister to him just as he did to Jeremiah and Elijah.

Is the journey too much for you at the moment? Has Happy become Weepy? Has your spouse let you down or a child turned against you? Have you seen a beloved friend end up being hurt or damaged by the church or mission? Are you struggling with your own personal disappointment or sense of failure? Maybe you are even second-guessing your decisions to be doing what you are doing.

If this is the case, how are you dealing with it all? Are you gun-shy of sharing your heart and hurt with anyone? Are you overwhelmed with sorrow? Let me assure you, you are not alone or unnoticed. Your tears are counted, your pain is registered in heaven, and your God is busy preparing to help you. As God provided food for Elijah, so he wants to provide food for you. In the word of the Lord we will find all of the strength we will need.

FACING GOD'S TRUTH

But how will this word of the Lord come to you? It may come directly from Scriptures, or as in Baruch's case, God may use another person to relay it. He used Jeremiah to speak to Baruch! Think about it. How humiliating for Baruch to have Jeremiah know what was going on inside, especially since some of what was going on had to do with his jealousy of Jeremiah and their respective roles! But it seems that Jeremiah did a sterling job of lovingly confronting his friend with God's truth while assuring him that he was just the messenger! This was not his criticism of his friend but God's evaluation of the situation.

I was waiting at an airport when my flight was canceled. There were about three hundred of us in the same predicament. The particular airline was operating on a go-slow protest order by the union. So you can imagine the tempers that were let loose when the hapless desk clerk had to make the bad-news announcement! I was amused to hear the way she did it. With an eye to self-preservation, she began delivering her piece of unwelcome news with the words, "Please, everybody, I am only the messenger!" I can hear Jeremiah assuring Baruch that this was the case, too!

We must understand that Baruch's testimony recorded in Jeremiah 45 was written after the fact. Baruch was not about to put anything that was going on inside him in writing! All this was part of his private pain, and as far as he was concerned, it was nobody's business but his own. If he had his way, it would stay private! Above all, he was not about to share it with his partner. Perhaps he didn't want the prophet to know how many regrets he was having! Maybe he didn't want to hurt him. But then God told on him! I can just hear Baruch saying, "Well now, that's great, Lord. Why did you have to do that?"

Years ago I was wrestling with some private pain. First my dad was diagnosed with cancer. Then God "added sorrow to my pain." We were in missions, and the work meant that my husband was traveling for the mission for long periods of time. I struggled with the sorrow over my dad and with constantly missing my husband, but I did not feel that I could tell anyone about it. After all, Joan, my senior missionary, was in the same situation, and she seemed to cope all right. She toughed it out just fine while I was becoming increasingly like Baruch, hiding my feelings and turning a brave face to the world.

Actually, I became quite proud of the fact that nobody really knew what was going on inside me. I determined to keep it that way. I knew that God knew, but I had stopped talking to him about it. I believed that he had told my friend, the senior missionary's wife, merely to toughen up. I knew that would be the message for me as well.

As I nursed my growing resentment against the mission, and obliquely against God, for putting me in this situation with seemingly no way out, God told on me! Somehow he let someone know about my pain. And guess who he told? That's right, my senior missionary! The very person I didn't want to know. I remember saying, as Baruch must have said, "Well now, that's great! Lord, why did you do that?"

The first thing the missionary said to me, however, was, "I'm just the messenger!" She managed to relay to me, as I believed Jeremiah managed to relay to Baruch, that this was not her word, but God's. She was not criticizing me; in fact, she had every sympathy for me. She, more than anyone else, understood my feelings. She was simply the mouthpiece of the Lord. The message was a tough one, as tough as the message to Baruch: "This is how it is; sometimes following Jesus brings with it a cost, but a cost, however much it hurts, that is eminently worth it!" My "bishop" used her staff to poke this soldier back into the fray.

The main thing Joan taught me was to not allow pain and sorrow to stop me from talking to God. "Why cut yourself off from your main source of help, Jill?" she asked me that day. The day I was able to receive that word of the Lord from my friend was the day I stumbled back to the throne room and was on my way to victory!

I realized she was only the messenger and that what she had to say was truth from God, so I was able to accept her words and do something about them. That day I asked God to take my resentment and anger and to help me have a sweet spirit of acceptance. *Chip, chip, chip!* There it was again, the sound of the chisel! God's instrument chipping away a bit more of that marble core of my selfishness.

Jeremiah must have been as reluctant to tell his friend the message God gave him as his friend was to receive it. How would you have felt if God gave you such a job? I am reminded of Samuel, who, when barely a teenager, was asked to tell the high priest, Eli, that God was not at all impressed with his fathering (I Samuel 3:11-21). God instructed the young boy to tell the aged priest that his two sons, Hophni and Phineas, were sons of the devil. He also had to tell Eli that because he had not restrained his sons, he and his sons would not live much longer. A tall order for a twelve-year-old, don't you think? Yet the boy Samuel was able to relay that difficult message to the old priest, who accepted the judgment of the Lord and simply said, "He is the Lord." Somehow Samuel knew how to pass along God's truth while saying, "I'm just the messenger."

Sometimes God asks us as parents or leaders to be the bearers of such messages. We need to make sure, like Samuel and Jeremiah, that we are hearing God's instructions correctly. We need to pray that we will be able to relay that vital piece of information in a way it will be accepted. We can start by saying, "I'm only the messenger!"

I think all the correction that Jeremiah had taken from God served him well when he faced Baruch with the Lord's message. I believe he was gentle and able to relay the message with grace. He had prayed, "So correct me, Lord, but please be gentle. Do not correct me in anger, for I would die" (Jeremiah 10:24, NLT). Gentleness is a grace we need to develop to do this most delicate work of rebuke and correction. So if you can't be gentle because you are too angry or for any other reason, I suggest you wait awhile.

But what if you are Baruch and not Jeremiah? Perhaps instead of delivering the hard message you have to receive it. The scribe apparently took it as truth from the Lord because he was still with Jeremiah in Egypt at the end of his life. What was the essence of his problem? What had brought him to this place of regret? What truths from God was he having to face in this difficult time? What are some of the truths you may have to face during your times of suffering?

The Truth about Your Pain

Baruch was sick of constant crises, of things never getting any better. "Woe to me! The Lord has added sorrow to my pain," he laments

(Jeremiah 45:3). He was nursing real resentment against the Lord. His first complaint had been that there was no letup. He endured pain only to meet more pain. Unrelenting crisis after crisis had worn him down. You can be worn out *in* the work of the Lord or you can be sick *of* the work of the Lord, and there is a difference! He had no recourse left. Worn down with sorrow and pain, he, like Jeremiah, began to get God and life mixed up. Notice that he said *the Lord* had added sorrow to his pain. But no, it wasn't the Lord; it was the Jewish leaders and King Nebuchadnezzar. It was life after the Fall that was the problem. It was Jeremiah's family, his family, and the opposition of all the political and religious leaders of the country who were adding sorrow to his pain. He had gotten God and life mixed up.

We may have to face God's truth about our pain—it is real, but we must be careful not to get God and life mixed up. God does not cause the pain and sorrow. He suffers with us and desires to comfort us as only he can.

The Truth about Yourself

Baruch was sick of himself. "I am weary of my own sighing and can find no rest" (Jeremiah 45:3, NLT). I think Baruch was disappointed with God and disappointed with himself for being disappointed with God!

I know little that irritates me more than me! I have kicked myself for a sharp tongue, quick judgments, rude answers, lack of faith, impatience, covetousness, boasting, and a whole lot more garbage that has worn me out. There is nothing quite as sickening as being sick of yourself! Baruch could not get a handle on himself. He was defeated by defeat in an area of his life and had decided to live with it. I did that when I was teaching school in Liverpool.

I had an overcrowded classroom of six-year-olds and little patience. Day after day something would happen in my classroom that would be the last straw, and I would lose it. Then I would come home and shut myself in my room, fall on my knees, and confess my impatience and bad temper. I would beg God to help me to do better the next day. The next day, however, was no better.

Despite my best intentions, a minor crisis would arise in the classroom, and I would blow it all over again! I was worn out with it. In the end I decided I would never get the better of my temper so I would just live with defeat. As long as no one saw what was going on, I could nurse my disappointment and feel miserable on the inside while being cheerful enough on the outside. But that is a miserable state of affairs! Baruch describes the sick feeling as "groaning." He felt isolated in his misery, and God felt far away.

Job describes a similar experience. "Even today my complaint is bitter; his hand is heavy in spite of my groaning. If only I knew where to find him; if only I could go to his dwelling!" (Job 23:2-3). Job, like Baruch, was getting God and life mixed up. And he was mad at himself for doing it!

Maybe you are thoroughly defeated in an area of your Christian life and you have given up. Maybe you are hoping that you can get away with this sorry state of affairs and no one will find out. Giving up, however, wears you down more than struggling. There seems no way Baruch can find an answer to his dilemma.

I know I thought there was no way out of my dilemma at the school. In the end this miserable schoolteacher tuned into what God was trying to say to me. It was the same message he gave to Baruch, and it was very simple, "I will protect you wherever you go" (Jeremiah 45:5, NLT). In other words, God said to me, "I am on your side." I learned that God was not the enemy. The kids were not the enemy. He would save me *in* the situation if I listened and obeyed him, but he was not going to save me *out of* the situation! As he helped me get a handle on my frustration, I began to learn self-control. Not all at once, but little by little, morning by morning, and day by day. Grace by grace his faithfulness to me eventually saved me from myself.

What is the truth about yourself? What do you need to face in your life? Have you given up? Are you trying to hide? Listen to God's words to Baruch, "I will protect you wherever you go." God is on your side. There's no use hiding. Take it to God, and let him lovingly help you deal with it.

The Truth about Pride

Baruch was sick of people's judgmental attitudes. Self-pity is really inverted pride, and pride was really at the root of Baruch's problem. God knew it, and he told Jeremiah, so Jeremiah knew it, too. Now everyone who reads the Bible knows it. So much for Baruch's hiding!

But this is the neatest thing about this whole chapter. Who wrote chapter 45? That's right, Baruch himself. He wanted everyone in the whole world to know God loved him so much that he refused to let Baruch wallow in his misery. God rescued him from the destruction that raw pride and selfishness had brought into his life. He didn't need to write chapter 45; he could have left it out. But he believed his lesson was so valuable for us all that he made sure he humbled himself enough to share it!

Pride was at the root of Baruch's misery, and pride is usually at the root of ours: "Are you seeking great things for yourself? Don't do it!" (Jeremiah 45:5, NLT). God saw ungodly ambition deep down in Baruch's heart. Living with other people's criticism is one thing, but living with God's criticism is quite another!

I have tried to copy Baruch's example. I seek to be completely honest with others. I share my failures, like losing my temper at school. I write about my down times in my books and relate them in meetings. I make sure if I need to pen a chapter 45, I pen it. I want people to understand that the way to "up" is "down" and that God will not leave us struggling with defeat! He will "give us life" as he gave it to Baruch. "Wherever you go I will let you escape with your life" (Jeremiah 45:5).

What are you seeking for yourself? Maybe you feel it is a holy ambition you hold close to your heart. You would like to do great things for God, but you would like to do them your way. You really want to call the shots, be in charge. You want to make decisions. Perhaps you feel you are in a backwater and are locked into working at half your capacity. Or maybe there is simply raw pride running rampant all over your life and you are coveting someone else's position, gift, or calling.

Pride has many faces. It says, "I want what you've got!" Or "I'm worth something more than this. I'm not appreciated, affirmed, congratulated, or rewarded for all my labor of love, and I'm sick of it. What's more, I want out." Pride is self at its worst and always stops you from being your best for God.

Pride will wear you down because pride puts you out there alone. Pride says, "I can do this alone. I don't need anyone's help, not even God's. And if I can't handle it, then I'll live with defeat rather than ask for help." Pride leaves you "playing God," and that will surely wear you out! Even the most natural activities, such as being a mother, can be an arena for self to flex its muscles and pride to rear its ugly head. Pride flexes its mother muscles and attempts to show the world just what it can do.

I remember trying to play God as a mother and quickly coming to the realization that I couldn't. Try as I might, I fell short of being omnipresent, omnipotent, and omniscient. After all, that was God's job, not mine! It was completely exhausting to be in all places at all times, be all powerful, and know everything that was going on in my kids' lives—but it didn't mean I didn't try! God hates pride because it is an attempt to do without him, to be independent and say, "I'll be my own God in my own garden and eat the fruit of my own labors." Shades of Eden! Whenever we insist on doing this, we are seeking great things for ourselves. God says to us, "Seek them not." Pride is self at its worst!

Maybe you secretly want to head up a women's ministry in your church. You would love to be asked to a position of leadership or be put in charge of arrangements for the Christmas program. You may think you have the skills and training to write a best-selling book, but no one has asked you to, no one has given you a break. The publishers always ask someone else—some Jeremiah who is younger and less experienced than you. Why has no one recommended you to speak at a large meeting or be invited to give the address at a church event?

If this is the case, try listening to whatever God is saying to you at this time in this situation. Be in his Word, and be alert to his voice—whether that voice addresses you directly, through circumstances, or through a trusted servant. Learn to tune in to the still small voice of conscience alerted by the prompting of the Spirit in your heart! I have a good example of allowing pride to rule in my own life. I want to do what Baruch did and share the way God was faithful in dealing with me. God is not about to let those he loves get away with pride.

There was a time in the early days of my Christian experience when people began to invite me to give my testimony. I was at first terrified to speak in public, but then the more I did it, the more I began to enjoy it. Subtly the devil fed my ego, and I began to want very much to be the one chosen to give my testimony. This, of course, was exacerbated by the devil, who needed only a foothold and was soon trampling all over my life. It wasn't long before I not only wanted to do it but also began resenting others who were asked instead of me. I really felt that I was better at it and had a better "story" to tell!

By this time I had met Stuart, who was preaching at various meetings around the country in his spare time. I was invited to go along with him and tell my story before he spoke. One day we were speaking at a Youth for Christ rally in my hometown of Liverpool. I sat on the platform and realized that I liked being up there. I hoped my face was shining for Jesus!

Soon it was time for the offering. I put my hand in my pocket and realized I had forgotten my money. Because pride was in my heart and I was way out of touch with God, I told a lie. It was a body-language lie. I put my hand in my pocket and pretended I had money in my hand and put it into the bucket. The bucket was being held in front of me by a young Youth for Christ worker, about fifteen years old.

He looked in the bucket, and so did I. What I didn't know was that there was no money in the bucket as nobody on the platform had put anything in! They, like me, must have forgotten their cash, too! So now, being thoroughly flustered, I proceeded to tell another "lie." I pretended my offering had dropped on the floor. At this, the bewildered young usher actually got down on his hands and knees to look for the nonexistent money! Not wanting him to be alone, I joined him! There we were, groveling around together underneath the chairs in full view of an interested crowd of people, searching for something that I knew full well did not exist. "Go on, go on," I hissed at the startled youth. He got up hastily and, not a little confused, continued down the row.

I sat down in my seat again and felt like throwing up! Then the Lord began to speak to me. I knew exactly what he was saying. *After this is over you must find this young man and tell him what you did.* I was horrified.

"But, Lord," I remonstrated, "what if he is a new Christian? Would this disillusion him to know someone who was giving her testimony behaved in such a way?"

Leave his reactions to me, said the Lord. *You follow me!*

I can't remember the rest of the meeting. I have no idea what I said or what my fiancé preached on. All I remember is feeling terrible about the whole affair.

At the end of the meeting I found the young man in question and took him behind the curtain on the stage. I told him what I had done and asked him to forgive me for making him look foolish in front of all those people. He looked at me solemnly and then said, "Can I pray for you?" which he promptly proceeded to do! As you can imagine, I was duly humbled and made a note that this young man, who had showed considerable maturity, should be the one to give his testimony next time instead of me. That is, if I were ever asked to do it again.

God showed me that day, as he showed Baruch, that I was seeking great things for myself and I was not to do it anymore. He would have nothing to do with such an attitude. He could neither use me nor bless me with such foolishness, and he would always find me out! "Great is his faithfulness" not only to make sure he helps me but also that he corrects and rebukes me. A child that is never corrected will think that his actions have no consequences. And if his actions have no consequence, then *he* has no consequences.

Is God pointing out pride in your life? If God is correcting you, it is because he loves you!

PUTTING HIS HURT IN YOUR HEART

After pointing out Baruch's pride, the Lord showed him his mistake. Baruch was thinking only of his own ministry. He had forgotten that his ministry was God's. The Lord began to show Baruch his self-centered heart and his tunnel vision. God was feeling terrible about the sin and godlessness in Israel. He wanted Baruch to be more concerned about God's pain and spoiled plans than his own.

"I will overthrow what I have built and uproot what I have planted. . . . I will bring disaster on all people" (Jeremiah 45:4-5). God's heart was broken because he was about to "abandon" the nation he loved "into the hands of her enemies" (Jeremiah 12:7).

Until we get around to feeling God's "hurt in our heart," we will never please him by our service. God doesn't want us to do our thing for him but rather let him do his thing for us.

Sometimes God helps us feel his pain as we feel our own pain. When I felt our son's pain after his wife left him, I glimpsed a fragment of the pain God feels when his people are unfaithful to him. Obviously, our son felt it more keenly than I did, and the pain we feel is, of course, infinitesimal compared to God's, but it helps to share it anyway. Glancing to heaven as I agonized over our child's hurts, I sensed that God was smiling at me in complete understanding.

God had told Jeremiah to write about his feelings when Israel committed spiritual adultery. "Does a maiden forget her jewelry, a bride her wedding ornaments? Yet my people have forgotten me, days without number. How skilled you are at pursuing love!" (Jeremiah 2:32-33). The Lord knows what it feels like when a spouse takes off her wedding band. " 'Like a woman unfaithful to her husband, so you have been unfaithful to me, O house of Israel,' declares the Lord" (Jeremiah 3:20). When I felt our son's pain over this, I understood a little of God's intense pain when we are unfaithful to him.

Chiseled by my children's choices—chiseled by their pain
Feeling I can hardly breathe or ever smile again!
Daring not to glance at Heaven and see my Father frown
Yet looking anyway, to see compassion smiling down.

God wants his hurt in our hearts and his tears on our face. God wants us to have the same huge compassion for his obdurate people as he has. This will obliterate all of our own selfish ambitions. God wants us to have an understanding of his heartbroken love for the world. He wants us to get on board with his plan for the redemption of the world and feel his compassion. This way we will be humbly grateful to play whatever part he chooses in the larger scheme of things.

KNOWING JESUS IS ALL YOU NEED

"You can't say Jesus is all you need until Jesus is all you've got," said Mother Teresa. This wonderful woman, who gave her life to the dying and destitute in India, could say that. Jesus was indeed all she had! She knew the truth of Jesus' words, "Is not life more important than food, and the body more important than clothes?" (Matthew 6:25).

Baruch was assured that his life would be saved in the coming disaster. "I will bring disaster on all people, declares the Lord, but wherever you go I will let you escape with your life" (Jeremiah 45:5). His life was the most important thing in the world. Passion, position, or possessions mattered little in the end. God promised him his life, and that was all. In other words, he said to Baruch, "It's not a fair world, Baruch, but at least you can be glad you have your life!"

God promised to save Baruch's life and nothing more. He uses a phrase that describes his life as "a prize of war," the booty a victorious army extracts from its victims. The word describes someone stripping prisoners of war of all their belongings before taking them off into slavery. As I watched the Serbs stripping the Albanians at the height of the Kosovo crisis, I understood a little of the meaning of this word. Even the people's passports and their legal identification, along with their landholding deeds and valuables, were stripped from them at the border crossings.

God warns Baruch that this will happen to him, but he promises that he will escape with his life. Baruch was to experience what the apostle Paul was to know years later. "Through glory and dishonor, bad report and good report; genuine, yet regarded as impostors; known, yet regarded as unknown; dying, and yet we live on; beaten, and yet not killed; sorrowful, yet always rejoicing; poor, yet making many rich; having nothing, and yet possessing everything" (2 Corinthians 6:8-10). Reduced to grace, down to God alone, God was going to be "God enough."

Now it was Baruch's time to respond to all of this divine attention. I believe there comes a time when God confronts us all with the choice that Baruch had at this point. Jeremiah had come to his grand submission in Jeremiah 10:23, saying, "I know, O Lord, that a man's life is not his own; it is not for man to direct his steps." So I believe Baruch repented of his pride and his ambition, made peace with Jeremiah, and set off at his side to finish the fight and keep the faith.

Would we have had the wonderful words of Jeremiah if Baruch had not surrendered his everything to God? If he had left Jeremiah and returned to the palace and his other world? I, for one, am grateful that he passed the test and soldiered on!

What a shout of joy the watching angels must have sounded at that moment! They knew that God is never limited by age, gender, culture, nationality, wealth, poverty, education, or lack of it. Only our pride, prejudice, sheer selfishness, and refusal to submit to the call of God in our lives can limit what God can do through us. *Chip, chip, chip* went the chisel. Baruch lay still in the Master's hand and looked a little bit more like his Master at the end of that day.

"Count on me if you need me, Lord," I can hear him say. "Call on me when it's rough. As long as you give me your grace to go on day by daily day, your faithfulness will see me through. I will bank on it, Lord, morning by morning and day by day."

Chiseled by my secret pride I choose not to confess
Sobered by your knowing that my life's so passionless
Shaped by all my sad regrets that cause you so much grief
Chiseled by my secret sin and shallow unbelief!

TIME OUT

These worksheets can be used in groups, in church classes, or with individuals as a discipling tool. They can also be used in a personal quiet time.

Take Time

1. Read Jeremiah 45, and write a brief summary. If you are working in a group, share your summary with the others.
2. How do you handle private pain? Like Jeremiah or like Baruch?
3. If appropriate, share an experience when God spoke to you concerning a pride issue through the word of some other "messenger."
4. Read the following references, and make a list of all you discover about pride.

   - Psalm 10:4
   - Psalm 62:10
   - Proverbs 8:13
   - Proverbs 11:2
   - Proverbs 13:10
   - Proverbs 16:18

5. Read 2 Chronicles 26:16-22. Discuss this story of one man's downfall through pride.

Prayer Time

1. Pray for people who are bearing private pain and have no one with whom to share it.
2. Pray for the Jeremiahs who have a ministry of "messenger."
3. Pray for the Baruchs in this world who are struggling with sorrow added to their pain.
4. Pray for the persecuted church around the world.
5. Pray for those whom God allows to go through trials.
6. Pray that God would show you how to have a ministry of confrontation with grace.

A Letter to God
Write a letter to God about your private pain.

CHAPTER NINE

FAITH THAT PERSEVERES

❧

HIS STRENGTH FOR YOUR DAYS

Take another scroll and write on it all the words
that were on the first scroll.
JEREMIAH 36:28

IF BARUCH HAD NOT COME TO A PLACE OF TOTAL SUB-
mission to God and the plans God had for his life and ministry, he
would never have been ready for the huge test that lay ahead of him.
Each act of obedience that God requires of us is important. Victory
today readies us for victory tomorrow. If we overcome a habit today, we are better able to overcome a habit tomorrow.

One of the biggest tests of my life was to tell my friends at college
that I had become a Christian. Converted during a stay in the hospital, I arrived back at my college dorm and tried to figure out the best
time to break what I knew would be unwelcome news. After reflection, there seemed to be no best time! It was going to be a shock
whenever they heard that the wildest girl of the bunch had "gone religious." I struggled with the thought of opening my brand-new Bible from Jenny in front of my friends. I knew I should pray by my
bed, but I couldn't bring myself to bow my reluctant knees in that
confined space and face the music. At the root of all of this was the
fear of losing my friends.

When I voiced my concerns to Jenny, she asked me, "What sort
of friends are they anyway, Jill, if they ditch you because you have
made your peace with God? Anyway, if you do lose them, God will
give you new friends who love the Lord." But I didn't want new
friends; I wanted my old ones!

DIFFICULT CHOICES

One fateful day I tremblingly got down on my knees with my brand-new Bible open on the bed in front of me. I couldn't pray! All I could do was will myself to stay there as my best friend looked at me in shock. Then I heard the door open, and she called out to the girls down the corridor, "Come here and look at this! She's gone cuckoo!" As I heard the footsteps coming along the corridor to "look at this," a huge sense of joy engulfed me. I think joy is feeling God's pleasure.

So many people think joy is experiencing their own pleasure. But it doesn't work like that. When we bring joy and delight to the heart of God, he lets us know that deep down inside us, and our heart smiles. When Jesus sent the larger group of his disciples out to minister in his name for the first time, they returned full of excited stories of what had happened. They also "returned with joy" (Luke 10:17). "Jesus, full of joy through the Holy Spirit, said, 'I praise you, Father, Lord of heaven and earth, because you have hidden these things from the wise and learned, and revealed them to little children. Yes, Father, for this was your good pleasure' " (Luke 10:21). When we are doing the Father's good pleasure—the things he has called and gifted us to do—his joy is transferred to our hearts, strengthening us to please him. After all, "the joy of the Lord is your strength" (Nehemiah 8:10). When Olympic sprinter Eric Liddell ran, he experienced the joy of God. "God made me fast, and when I run, I feel his pleasure," he said.

As I knelt there by my bed in college, I felt his pleasure, too. I knew I was exactly where I ought to be, doing what I should be doing. It would be all right, even though I was sure this was the end of those friendships. I was right about that. My friends never spoke to me again, and I was left to find out whether God would give me other friends. I know now that if I had not passed that basic test, I would not have been ready for the next one, and the next, and the next.

So much hinged on Baruch's decisions. If he had not left his palace and taken his stand with Jeremiah in the first place, he would not have been ready for the next test—facing his friends in the temple with the truth. Whatever small challenge you are facing as a Christian in a hostile world, never underestimate its importance. God is strengthening you along the way for the bigger challenges ahead.

It might be that you do his will and your heart smiles but other hearts frown, or worse, scowl! You may feel God's pleasure while others are incensed. In the same passage that Jesus talks about the disciples knowing his joy and their joy being full, he talks about the world hating them (John 17:13-14). The forces of evil are not moved by our joy. In fact, their fury knows no bounds when they come across joyful Christians, and they set about wiping the joy off our faces. They do this by entering the arena of our testing and trying to use it to their advantage. But God is on our side, and we shall not be moved, even in the greatest trials. Undoubtedly Jeremiah and Baruch were about to endure one of the biggest tests, so let's see how they coped.

Dietrich Bonhoeffer was a German pastor who, in the face of Nazism, said, "When a person has completely given up the idea of making something of himself—then one throws himself entirely into the arms of God, then one no longer takes seriously his own sufferings, but rather the suffering of God in the world" (*Broadman's Commentary on John*, p. 372).

Bonhoeffer took his prison term as a gift of God to him and an opportunity to minister to other victims in the prison. Bonhoeffer lost his life to gain it in a better place. He became so identified with the "fellowship of Christ's sufferings" that his life stands as a beacon and an example for the suffering church around the world. He learned Baruch's lesson. Baruch came to the same point—giving up the idea of making something of himself. He passed the test, focusing on the things that mattered to God and not the things that mattered to him, and buckled down to the task in hand.

TOUGH CIRCUMSTANCES

Jeremiah and Baruch continued their work with the word of God, and the opposition did their level best to silence them, even putting Jeremiah under house arrest. They did not, however, confine

Baruch. Perhaps Baruch's friends put in a good word for him. Maybe there were more sympathetic people in the government than we know about who could pull a few strings. In any case, surely God's hand kept Baruch free for the job he wanted him to do. Having Jeremiah confined to his quarters did not stop the men from doing their work. In fact, it was in this restricted situation that they accomplished their work, and the precious scrolls were written.

I think of the apostle Paul in prison saying, "What has happened to me has really served to advance the gospel" (Philippians 1:12). Would the prison epistles have been written without the prison? Hardly. Imagine doing without the book of Philippians! Would the book of Jeremiah be in our Bible today if Jeremiah had remained a free man? Jeremiah and Baruch learned to see an opportunity in every difficulty and used their time of forced inactivity to good advantage.

Do you find yourself confined to the house? Do you feel as if you are under house arrest? You can feel like that if you have small children and you are a stay-at-home mom. You can identify if you are fighting a chronic disease and you are home for a long recuperation. Perhaps you are a caregiver and restricted by your responsibilities. There are myriad ways you can understand the feelings of Jeremiah and Baruch. There is so much to do, and yet you have been put under house arrest! Use the time. If God wanted you out and about, you would be out and about. The Lord gave the two men a gift of grace when he gave them this period of forced confinement.

I remember feeling as though I was under house arrest when I was a young mother and my husband was traveling. I was shut up for endless days and nights in a small house with three children below school age. One day in the middle of my quiet time a still small voice said, *It's a gift. Why don't you say thank you?* If I had failed the test of treating this period of time as a privilege rather than as a punishment, I would have missed the opportunity to begin to develop my writing skills. Looking back, I have never since had such a sweet time of productivity. Listen to God's voice. He is saying, "It's a gift!"

God gave the gift of "house arrest" to Jeremiah, and he accepted it and exploited it for the Lord. "Take a scroll and write on it all the words I have spoken to you concerning Israel, Judah and all the other nations from the time I began speaking to you in the reign of Josiah till now," the Lord instructed Jeremiah (Jeremiah 36:2). So the two servants of the Lord used the tough circumstance of arrest as a time to work hard to finish the scrolls. Jeremiah had to remember, perhaps with the help of notes, twenty years' worth of messages, and Baruch painstakingly wrote them down.

GOD ENABLES

That was twenty years of memories—a lot of words on a scroll and a lot of remembering! If I had been Jeremiah, I can imagine how many excuses I would have made. I have written a few autobiographical books and know how hard it is to remember that many years back. I have said, as I'm sure Jeremiah did, "Lord, I can't remember. Help me." And God himself brought the necessary words and incidents to mind.

Have you ever had a hard time remembering things? Have you said, "But, Lord, I can't possibly remember all those things. What happens if I get it wrong?" Yet God himself enables us to fulfill all of his demands. If you, like Jeremiah and Baruch, simply are obedient to whatever God is asking of you, you will find you have the capacity to do it.

The Bible simply records the men's obedience. "So Jeremiah called Baruch son of Neriah, and while Jeremiah dictated all the words the Lord had spoken to him, Baruch wrote them on the scroll" (Jeremiah 36:4). Together they accomplished this incredible task. What seemingly impossible thing has God called you to do? Do you know that God himself by his enabling Spirit will do it? "The one who calls you is faithful and he will do it" (1 Thessalonians 5:24).

Facing a big writing project that asked for daily Bible study notes for a year, I felt overwhelmed and quite inadequate. I sat miserably in my study, berating myself for taking on the assignment. It required remembering many things from the past. Bible notes were lost, outlines of sermons long gone, and yet these were the very things I needed to do the job. "I can't remember enough," I complained to the Lord. "I should have been better organized and kept better files. I'm old, and it's hard to remember all those verses and lessons of the past."

You are as old as you should be, he reminded me. *You certainly should have kept better notes, but you didn't.*

"So what shall I do now? I can't remember!" I whined.

I can remember, he replied. *Ask me! I called you to this task, now rely on me to do the work in you and through you.* And God enabled me to remember. I finished the project and, incidentally, with material left over!

As the two men took the opportunity to work on the scrolls, Nebuchadnezzar was marching toward their city. Yet Jeremiah and Baruch never gave up. They didn't throw their hands up and say, "What's the use? It's all over," or, "Well, these obdurate people have had their chances to hear Jeremiah's preaching. Why should we believe they would read his book?" They had faith enough to try one more thing, take one more risk, and finish the work they were doing. They had faith enough to believe that it is never over till it's over.

DON'T GIVE UP

As they worked, they prayed for the people to whom they were writing. Jeremiah's prayers fill his writings. They permeate his work, and he included them in his manuscript. If you want to learn how to pray for hard-hearted people, study the prayers of Jeremiah. If you want to learn how to pray for yourself, look into the prayer life of this man. The two men prayed stubbornly, consistently, and with perseverance that the people of God would yet repent so that God would relent in sending disaster.

God's intent is always to offer people every possible chance to come back to him. Jeremiah and Baruch knew that. They believed that "his compassions never fail. They are new every morning" (Lamentations 3:22-23). "Perhaps when the people of Judah hear about every disaster I plan to inflict on them, each of them will turn from his wicked way; then I will forgive their wickedness and their sin," God tells them (Jeremiah 36:3). Because Jeremiah believed it was never over till it was over, he labored on.

Have you given up on someone? Have you quit praying for her? Has she given you little hope of her turning back to the Lord? Listen, it's never over till it's over. Call her on the phone one more time. Invite her to church. Send her that book or tape. Do battle on your knees for her. Weep before the throne. That person may yet repent, even if Nebuchadnezzar is knocking at the door. Jesus said that we "should always pray and not give up" (Luke 18:1). We must not give up. Jesus said so.

HAVE A HEART

We should also be strategic and intentional. Perhaps Jeremiah thought the written word could have more impact than the spoken word. Sometimes that is the case. Anyway, he chose a fast day when there would be plenty of people around. He gave the precious scroll to his friend, saying, "I cannot go to the Lord's temple. So you go to the house of the Lord on a day of fasting and read to the people from the scroll the words of the Lord that you wrote as I dictated" (Jeremiah 36:5-6).

It's always a good idea to choose strategic times and places to preach the Word. It's no good fishing in a swimming pool! Why do we put on gospel services inside the four walls of a church and insist on preaching to the choir? We must go where the fish are, which is usually outside church boundaries. And we need to go out to them and not expect them to come to us. Jeremiah didn't say to Baruch, "Go and bring the officials and some of the people here to me." He asked, "How can we make the maximum impact in as short a time as possible?"

In the seventies the churches in England were virtually empty. Certainly there were a few young people around, but we would have waited forever if we had waited for the "fish" to swim into our churches and give themselves up! The time was short, and the days were evil. It took a few church people to think of radical ways to reach a lost generation. It was easy once we thought about it. When you go fishing, you go where the fish are! So we did.

Two evenings a week we went into the coffee bars, dance halls, fairgrounds, and anywhere else there was a crowd, telling the Word any way people would listen. Sometimes we spoke the Word, sometimes we read it out loud, often we would use music and drama, and sometimes we spread the message in the form of Bibles or tracts. And we learned like Jeremiah that holidays (or feast days) were excellent times to take the Word of God to a crowd.

Of course, all the planning and effort are a lot more trouble than joining a church and paying a pastor to do all of the work! All too often we leave this sort of outreach to the "professional" Christian or the trained layperson. Baruch could have easily refused to take on the role of chief spokesperson and simply said he would pray about it. But there is a place for "ordinary" believers to articulate their faith. Every Christian is to be a witness to what he or she knows about the truth and the One of whom the truth speaks.

When Jesus told his disciples that they were to be witnesses "in Jerusalem, and in all Judea and Samaria, and to the ends of the earth" (Acts 1:8), he was talking to fishermen, tax collectors, and businessmen. Baruch knew that his main gift was writing, but his main responsibility was to assist in any way he could to get the word of God to the people. The motivation was to have a heart for the Lord and for the people. Baruch had allowed God to grow a heart like that in him. Now God would put that heart to the test.

Jeremiah chose a holiday time to read the precious scrolls. He wanted to make sure the messages achieved maximum impact. It was certainly a whole lot of trouble to go to the people instead of expecting them to come to him, but nothing will be too much trouble if you have a heart for the people!

Jeremiah definitely had a heart for the people, as did Baruch. In one of his messages the prophet says, "Hear and pay attention, do not be arrogant, for the Lord has spoken. . . . But if you do not listen, I will weep in secret because of your pride; my eyes will weep bitterly, overflowing with tears, because the Lord's flock will be taken captive" (Jeremiah 13:15-17). Having a heart for the people means that you weep in secret for them, that your tears talk.

> *Tears talking, pattering petition on the door of Heaven; let me in.*
> *God opens the front door, and I enter the house of prayer.*
> *I have company of course; my friend the intercessor waits for me.*
> *"My intercessor is my friend as my eyes pour out tears to God."*
> *(Job 16:20)*

As we develop a viable prayer life in the secret places of the heart, we should not be surprised to hear our "tears talking." The prayer life that is viable is a prayer life that affects the heart—and our tear ducts.

I have never been involved in any effective evangelism program that has not been preceded by prayer. Billy Graham says the three rules of effective evangelism are: prayer, prayer, and prayer! Jeremiah had been doing this secret work of prayer for these stubborn people for a long time. Understanding that their problem was pride, he had been praying about that very thing. Jeremiah's prayers affected his heart and drove him on. The people's pride caused him to "weep bitterly" because he understood where it was taking them. "The Lord's flock will be taken captive" (Jeremiah 13:17).

SHED TEARS

When you read of Jesus weeping over Jerusalem, you hear his heart. You hear his tears talking: "How often I have longed to gather your children together, as a hen gathers her chicks under her wings, but you were not willing" (Matthew 23:37). We can pray about people's stubborn pride. Jesus and Jeremiah did.

Prayer that is effective is prayer that is specific. Jeremiah didn't get on his knees and pray fervently, "Bless Israel!" He got down to specifics. He prayed about the root problem, and he prayed about the repercussions of the problem. If we will be effective in our prayers, we must do our homework so we can intercede with an intelligent understanding of the situation.

Prayer also prepares the ground before the seed is scattered on it. The sowers scatter the seed, and our tears water it. Prayer is the place where God softens our hard hearts toward difficult people who may be giving the sowers a hard time. And our prayers soften their hearts, too.

Jeremiah prayed plenty of "I've had it with them" prayers. When he stayed in the presence of God long enough, however, he began to catch the heart of God for these same people, and soon he would be weeping for them instead of wanting vengeance. There is little hope of nursing a heart of vengeance if you are engaging in a viable prayer ministry. A heart for people is developed on your knees.

I am struck with Jeremiah's likeness to God. The prophet's heart yearned for the people to repent and turn to the Lord, just as Jesus' heart did. Jeremiah's troubles were chiseling him into the likeness of God. "Perhaps they will bring their petition before the Lord, and each will turn from his wicked ways, for the anger and wrath pronounced against this people by the Lord are great," he says (Jeremiah 36:7). God's tears were on Jeremiah's face. God's compassion was in Jeremiah's heart. God's mercy was evident in the words Jeremiah was praying. God's love was being offered freely to his people throughout Jeremiah's life.

The secret of a heart of compassion is a secret prayer life that no one else knows about. What are you and God secretly doing together? Are you talking to him regularly about all the people who are bound for destruction if they don't repent, or could you not care less? You don't grow compassion in public; you grow it on your face before God in the secret place.

Not long ago I spent some time asking God to show me an area of my devotional life in which he wanted me to grow. Unmistakably the answer came back, *I want you to care.*

"But I do care, Lord," I remonstrated. "I spend every living moment attending to your work."

Where are the tears? he asked me quietly. I had no answer because I had no tears. It was time to let him do his work in me in the secret places of my heart.

If there are no tears, I will not be standing in the temple courts on the day of fasting. I will not be putting my life on the line. I will not be taking risks, pushing boundaries, attaining heights, taking new initiatives. There will be no late-night candles burning at both ends because people are dying without Christ. Lamentations 3:22 says, "His compassions never fail." It doesn't say they "sometimes" fail but that they "never" fail!

Compassion moves you from the comparative safety of your own house into the marketplace of the world to shout out the message from the housetops. Compassion gets you off the evangelical donkey and into the ditch or, if you like, into the trenches. If you are moved with compassion, you don't ride past someone in trouble as the scribe or Pharisee did in Jesus' parable of the Good Samaritan (Luke 10:25-37). You get down from your high horse and attend to the one who has been robbed and beaten by thieves. We must not leave this sort of compassion to the Jeremiahs of this world. We all need to develop a heart for people.

What would have happened if Baruch had refused to let God break his heart? Jeremiah couldn't go preaching one day, so Baruch took his place. He wouldn't have done that if his spiritual eyes had been dry. This challenge is for everyone, speaker and scribe alike. Every Christian is called to be a witness with a heartfelt message.

WORK OUTSIDE YOUR GIFTING

When Jeremiah was put under house arrest, he realized he needed a messenger. His work was finished, and it was time to read the scroll to the people. He couldn't do it because he was imprisoned in his own house. Someone else would have to go for him. So Jeremiah did the obvious thing: He sent Baruch. "You can do it. I cannot go to the Lord's temple, but you can," I can hear him saying encouragingly to the scribe. "So you go to the house of the Lord on a day of fasting and read to the people from the scroll the words of the Lord that you wrote as I dictated" (Jeremiah 36:6).

Jeremiah had great confidence in his friend. He had spent hours of prayer with him, and he knew his heart. Jeremiah also knew that "heart" was more important than "gift." It would be Baruch's heart for the Lord and for the people that would give him the courage to go to the temple and work outside of his gifting. Baruch could have offered all sorts of excuses. Above all, he could have objected, "It's not my gift." But he didn't. He set off and just "did it."

Have you ever used the excuse that you can't do something that needs doing because it's not your gift? Have you had some really good teaching on spiritual gifts and been quite excited that you have actually discovered yours? The only danger in that is you might abdicate your responsibilities if you don't believe you are gifted for them! Maybe you have been exercising your gifts happily within the church or in the community. Then a need has arisen, and someone has asked you to volunteer to meet it. Have you ever said, "Sorry [you are really highly relieved], but it's not my gift"? Even if it is not your gift, it may still be your responsibility!

As a pastor's wife I have needed to listen to people's troubles and try to say something to help them. Some would call that counseling. I do not count this as one of my gifts. I do it because there are not enough ears to listen to the hurts out there. At the end of my teaching meetings people want to talk and ask questions. Often these talks turn into "counseling sessions." I find myself working outside of my gifting a lot of the time. At times like these I try to have a ministry of silence (listening) and a ministry of tears. Anyone can listen, and anyone can cry! That is, anyone who has asked God to break his or her heart with the things that break the heart of God. Only after I have tried to exercise a ministry of silence and tears do I use words. Try it. It is amazing the helpful thoughts that come to you in the silence. A talker like me needs to exercise self-control in order to be a good listener, but God is delighted to help you with this if you ask him to!

Baruch was willing to work outside of his gifting when it was necessary, and off he went with Jeremiah's talks on those precious scrolls.

HAVE A GO!

In Britain we have a saying: "Have a go!" It means you may not think you have a chance of making something work, but if the "something" is worth the chance, you should "have a go!" I have found Americans reticent about "having a go." If they can't do it well, they must not do it at all, or so the argument goes.

It takes more grace to say yes to such opportunities than it does to say no. It takes the grace of God to "have a go" at a spiritual challenge that seems totally beyond us. I have found, however, that in trying to meet needs that I have felt I was not qualified to meet, I have had to depend more on God. When I depend more on God, I receive even more grace than when I worked within my own gifting!

Shortly after coming to America and taking the pastorate, I found myself facing so many needs I thought I was not gifted for, and I became greatly discouraged. I wanted to go back to England! But we don't have the luxury of "going back to England" every time we feel discouraged! I realized I couldn't choose to respond only to the things I knew I could do well because I was gifted to do them. This was especially true in the area of evangelism. The need is so great that evangelism is a situation that requires "all hands on deck." The world is going to hell in a handbasket, and whether I am gifted or not, I can at least raise my voice above the noise and warn people where they are headed. My voice may not be pretty, but it can be loud! After all, if you see someone about to walk blindly over a cliff, it doesn't matter *how well* you shout to warn them of the danger but only *that* you shout!

Baruch, to his great credit, was willing to shout the message and to work outside his gifting when it was necessary. He was willing to lift up his voice for God and his cause. Like Jeremiah, he had allowed the Lord to grow compassion in the secret places of his heart. That compassion drove him to simple obedience and dependence on the great God of mercy whom he served.

Any one of us can do the same. If we can read, we can read the Word of God to people who need to hear it. If we can talk, we can speak the Word of God. Baruch took Jeremiah's life work and headed off to the temple to make sure it would get a hearing. The Bible simply says, "Baruch son of Neriah did everything Jeremiah the prophet told him to do; at the Lord's temple he read the words of the Lord from the scroll" (Jeremiah 36:8). Sweet! Angels sang, God smiled. By the incredible grace of God, people in Israel received one more chance to be saved.

USE YOUR INFLUENCE

Actually in this particular incident Baruch was God's ideal instrument of grace. He still wielded a lot of influence. Baruch could use a weapon that Jeremiah didn't have—influence in high places. He read the scroll from a room in the temple that belonged to a secret supporter. That was a clever move. Jesus said we are to be "as shrewd as snakes and as innocent as doves" (Matthew 10:16). So Baruch chose to call in a favor on a friendship. "From the room of Gemariah son of Shaphan . . . Baruch read to all the people" (Jeremiah 36:10).

Gemariah was the son of Shaphan, who had been Josiah's secretary of state (2 Kings 22:3). Gemariah's brother, Ahikam, was one of the few remaining friends of Jeremiah (Jeremiah 26:24). So this family was a godly family and most likely were open to Jeremiah's message. Baruch boldly asked for their help, and they allowed him to set up shop in the inner court of the temple. Baruch chose his contacts with care, and it paid off. Stationing himself in the doorway of his friend's room, he read some of the scroll to the people who had come to the day of fasting. Influence helps. Baruch was ready to use the influence he still had with erstwhile colleagues. We should not be afraid to invite such influence. We can pray about who might help us in our goal to get the word out.

Maybe you are not identifying with the prophet and the scribe but with the friendly officials. Is there a Jeremiah or a Baruch who desperately needs your influence and help? Perhaps someone needs a room to work in or access to vital information. If you have influence you could exercise, why not go out on a limb and help a young Jeremiah in his or her mission?

At a conference in the north of England I listened to the testimony of a businessman who had invited some young evangelists to dinner. These young men and women had a dream of reaching India by mobilizing students, equipping them for literature work, and driving all the way to India with donated vans full of Bibles to sell. It was a bold plan. The mission team members, led by a young American, were ready for the personal price they had to pay. They had nothing but faith, vision, and a stubborn love for the Lord. The businessman was fascinated with their spiritual nerve. "What can I do to help?" he asked them.

Well, he could give them a room in his house. He could use his influence. He could go to bat for them in the community. And he did. He became part of the founding board and then actually took out a mortgage on his own house to give the team a flying start. He was a Gemariah. He used his influence to launch one of the most exciting mission works in the world today. He put himself at risk to help a young Jeremiah get the Word of God out to the incredibly needy country of India. Today that mission distributes millions of Bibles around the world. Maybe you identify with Jeremiah, or with Baruch, or even with Gemariah. Everyone has a role to play in God's plan. We just need to make sure we each do our part.

As the not unsympathetic officials listened to the dire warnings communicated in the scrolls that Baruch was reading to them, they believed that Jeremiah's words were from God himself. Realizing they were of great public interest and significance, they shared them with a few more officials who also believed that the message they contained was true. "The king needs to hear this," they decided, and so off they went to the king. "When Micaiah son of Gemariah, the son of Shaphan, heard all the words of the Lord from the scroll, he went down to the secretary's room in the royal palace, where all the officials were sitting" (Jeremiah 36:11-12). He told them about the scrolls, and these officials asked Baruch to read to them as well. So he did, and they believed, too.

Aware of the obvious threat this posed for Baruch and Jeremiah, and anticipating the reaction of King Jehoiakim, they left the precious scrolls in the room of Elishama, the secretary, for safekeeping. Then they went and told the king. But the king, on hearing what the messages contained, demanded to read the scrolls for himself. So the officials reluctantly brought the scrolls to him. "The king sent Jehudi to get the scroll, and Jehudi brought it from the room of Elishama the secretary and read it to the king" (Jeremiah 36:21).

The leaders had already made sure that Jeremiah and Baruch were in hiding, which was just as well, as the king was about to put them out of the way for good. How God helped Jeremiah and Baruch escape from house arrest we don't know, but escape they did, for "the Lord had hidden them" (Jeremiah 36:26). I love that phrase. For when God hides a man, he *hides* a man!

Think of Elijah. When Ahab and Jezebel were after his life, God hid him in a ravine, and ravens brought him food (1 Kings 17:2-6). Did God use his creatures again to care for his servants Jeremiah and Baruch? We don't know. But it seems someone was willing to risk the consequences of hiding the two most-wanted men in Israel.

The king, meanwhile, was about to do away with the Word of the Lord altogether. He showed no spiritual interest at all in the powerful words on the scrolls and, in fact, was hostile and angry. It is incredible to me that Jehoiakim was the son of Josiah. How could a Josiah produce a Jehoiakim? Josiah had rediscovered the Word of God and demanded a public reading of it, after which he instituted religious reforms because of the powerful words it contained. And now here is his son about to treat the Word of God with contempt.

There are no guarantees that the next generation of believers will own their fathers' faith. Each person must make his or her own choice in this regard. Jehoiakim, despite his rich spiritual heritage, chose to turn his back on the God of his fathers and, worse, to go down the road to destruction—taking Israel with him.

Do It Again

What happened next almost defies description. Jeremiah, seemingly horrified at the actions of the king, took pains to record the details for us.

The king was sitting in the courtyard of the palace, and it was winter. Because it was cold, there was a charcoal fire burning in a firepot. As the king demanded that the scroll be read, he listened. Then taking a knife, he cut the piece of the message that was read from the scroll and threw it in the fire! The officials were horrified and bravely protested. But "even though Elnathan, Delaiah and Gemariah urged the king not to burn the scroll, he would not listen to them" (Jeremiah 36:25).

Baruch's colleagues' objections made no difference at all as "the king and all his attendants who heard all these words showed no fear, nor did they tear their clothes" (Jeremiah 36:24). Piece by precious piece, twenty years of work went up in flames! "The king cut them off with a scribe's knife and threw them into the firepot, until the entire scroll was burned in the fire" (Jeremiah 36:23). How could he do such a thing? It's hard to imagine anyone doing such a destructive thing today—or is it?

When my husband-to-be was in business, he worked in Manchester and lived in the YMCA. This brought him into contact with lots of students in that university town. One young man named John began to argue with him about Christianity.

John was having a lot of trouble believing that the Bible was the Word of God and that the messages from it were true. One day Stuart gave him a Bible and told him to take it away and read it through. He then handed him a pair of scissors and suggested he cut out of the text everything he could not (or, as Stuart suspected, *would not*) believe.

John was horrified. "Oh, I couldn't possibly do that!" he said.

"Why not?" inquired Stuart.

"Because it's the Bible, and it's sort of holy," John replied.

"Why can't you cut it up with scissors?" inquired Stuart. "You spend all the time I'm talking to you cutting it into shreds with your tongue!"

John got the point.

There are more ways of tearing up the truth than the king of Israel ever thought about. The end result, however, is the same. God is not amused! You can't treat the truth of God with impunity and escape the wrath of God! Take scissors or tongue and destroy the truth, and God will see to it you do not live to tell the tale! So what happened next?

Someone went to Jeremiah and Baruch and told them what had happened. Can you imagine their reaction? What would you have felt like if you received the news that your life's work had been destroyed? All that painstaking work up in smoke. Both men must have been absolutely crushed. Maybe they prepared to "go back to England" or, rather, to escape to the Babylonians. Surely it was all over. Whatever their reaction, I know they prayed about it. After they did that, the word of the Lord came to Jeremiah with perhaps the most amazing message of all: "Do it again! Just do it again!" The Bible says, "After the king burned the scroll containing the words that Baruch had written at Jeremiah's dictation, the word of the Lord came to Jeremiah: 'Take another scroll and write on it all the words that were on the first scroll, which Jehoiakim king of Judah burned up'" (Jeremiah 36:28). The word of the Lord "happened" to Jeremiah again, and surely this was the most profound "happening" in his entire life!

Would they have faith enough to finish? How would they respond to the voice of God? How would you have responded? Would you start all over again, or would you quit? Guess what Jeremiah and Baruch did: "Jeremiah took another scroll and gave it to the scribe Baruch son of Neriah, and as Jeremiah dictated, Baruch wrote on it all the words of the scroll that Jehoiakim king of Judah had burned in the fire" (Jeremiah 36:32).

Just like that! Jeremiah handed Baruch another scroll and began all over again! They did it again. Yes, they did it again! Now that's faithfulness! But can't you just hear the chisel and the hammer at work? *Chip, chip, chip,* as two men became a little bit more like the faithful God they served.

What is God saying to you? Have you quit the ministry? Is he saying to you, "Will you do it again for me?" Have you given up trying to influence your family for the Lord because the last time they tore you to shreds? Will you do it again for God? Have you grown so discouraged teaching an unruly group of teenagers at church that you have told the pastor you are taking a break? Will you "do it again"? What straw has broken the camel's back? Who tried to destroy your faith? Who ridiculed your beliefs? Who laughed at your lifestyle?

Read Jeremiah 36. Open your heart to what God is saying to you, and see what happens. If you do, I believe you will hear God say, "Take another scroll and start from the beginning." Or commit to another semester with those difficult teenagers. You may hear him ask you to burn the midnight oil writing curriculum or planning a women's event or teaching English as a second language. It could be one more letter you need to write to an estranged spouse or unruly teenager. I don't know what God's word to you will be, but I do know he wants to supply you with the grace to pick up your pen and scroll, whatever that represents, and just "do it again!"

For this you will need Jesus, but for this you *have* Jesus. He lives by his Spirit in your heart. You will have all that you need as the occasion arises to "do it again and again and again until it is done." Jeremiah and Baruch came through for us. Thanks to them we have the Word of the Lord. For whom do you need to come through? Perhaps you will never know, and that is not the issue. God knows whom he wants to benefit in the years to come by your example and your obedience as you "do it again."

The men's simple and immediate response to this staggering request of God challenges me mightily. Without a word of complaint they started over. That day, that very moment, they got to work, and God was with them every step of the way. Of course he was, for God always enables and empowers us for his own demands!

Moment by moment and day by daily day the work went on until it was finished. In fact, God instructed Jeremiah and Baruch to add many more words (Jeremiah 36:32). You can guess who those words were for, can't you? Yes, that's right, King Jehoiakim. For God was not amused!

TIME OUT

These worksheets can be used in groups, in church classes, or with individuals as a discipling tool. They can also be used in a personal quiet time.

Take Time

1. Read Jeremiah 36. Then read it again. What did you notice the second time that you did not notice the first time you read it?
2. Have you ever needed to remember the Word of God? How has God himself helped you to do it?
3. What do you think of the concept of going where the fish are? How can you put this concept to work in church? Brainstorm ideas.
4. Have you ever worked outside your gifting? What happened?
5. Define influence. List people within the sphere of your influence. With whom do you identify most—Jeremiah, Baruch, or Gemariah? Why?
6. Which is the most important element in ministry: gift or heart? Discuss.
7. How do we get a compassionate heart? Memorize Ephesians 4:32.
8. Do you think God was unreasonable to ask Jeremiah and Baruch to "do it again"? Can you identify? Share examples if appropriate.

Prayer Time

1. Talk to God about the chapter. Tell him what you liked about it and what you didn't. Tell him how it frightened you and how it challenged you. Write down a list of your fears. Pray about them one by one.
2. Pray for tears. Make a list of the things you think God wants you to care about.
3. Pray for compassionate ministries to flourish in your church. Write down some ideas you could try to get going. Ask: "Who

needs help? Can I supply it?" Make a list of the ideas you have thought about. Prioritize them.

4. Sit quietly and think of ways you have influence. Ask God how you can exploit those spheres of influence for him. Write down one person you could try to influence for the Lord this week.

5. Pray for all the people who need to "do it again." Pray for endurance and perseverance. Pray for missionaries. Pray for marriages. Pray for discouraged evangelists.

6. Pray for yourself and your family.

A Letter to God
Write a letter asking God to give you faith enough to finish whatever task he has given you, to do it again and again, until his work is accomplished.

CHAPTER TEN

FAITH ENOUGH TO FINISH

❧

I AM HEARD

Then you will call upon me and come and pray to me,
and I will listen to you. You will seek me and find me
when you seek me with all your heart.
JEREMIAH 29:12-13

ONE DAY AS I WAS FINISHING THIS WORK, I MET WITH GOD
to talk about what I had written. "Lord" I said, "I desire what I have
written to be a help to those who need 'faith enough to finish.'"

"I see your heart, Jill," the Lord replied. "I desire it to be of help,
too." Then I seemed to hear him asking me, "Has the work been a
help to you?"

"Yes, Lord," I answered. "I feel that Stuart and I are in the finishing stretch of our lives and ministry, so I have been trying to apply
the lessons to my own heart along the way."

"Good," he said, "because I want you to finish strong."

"Jeremiah had forty years of ministry, Lord. How many will we
have, do you think?" That sounded so silly because I knew he knew.
I just wondered if he would give me a hint about how close to the
finish line we were! After all, David had dared to ask the Lord the
same question: "Show me, O Lord, my life's end and the number of
my days; let me know how fleeting is my life" (Psalm 39:4). Or,
"Remind me that my days are numbered" (NLT).

"Are you worrying about your age again, Jill?"

"I suppose so," I muttered. And then I heard as clear as a bell,
"The span of my years is as nothing before you" (Psalm 39:5). I
wondered why, if my age was "as nothing" before him, it was so very

important to me! "I don't feel that I've had time to do all the things I want to do for you," I explained.

"I know the feeling," he said quietly. "At the end of three years of ministry I had finished the work the Father had given me to do. But there seemed to be so much left undone. But it's not a question of having time to do all the things *you* want to do for me but of having the time to do all the things *the Father* wants you to do for me! When those things are done, I will open the Front Door, and you can come in. But not before."

Then I remembered Jeremiah chapter 1! How could I have forgotten so soon? He knew me before I was me to know, and he put his work in my hands. My mind also went to Psalm 139:16: "All the days ordained for me were written in your book before one of them came to be." He had written down the number and had chosen to keep it his secret. It was for my good. It should be so. So I sat down with the manuscript and continued my dialogue.

My personal worry for quite a while had been, "Will we finish strong?" I had learned that we have to do our part. And what is our part? It is first and foremost to have a sense of "calling." When we can look up to heaven and say with understanding, "I want *your* plan in my life," and we commit to a relationship with God that takes first place before all our other relationships, then we will have begun to do our part. That relationship leads us to know the things he has in mind for us. To finish strong, we must nurture our relationship with him.

"Those things you have in mind for us, Lord," I commented, "those secondary callings that are the tasks and responsibilities you have prepared for us to do—those have not always been easy. And I have not always done them. Forgive me for that."

"I will," he said simply.

"Yet I have achieved some of them, I think," I added hopefully.

"Some," he agreed. "Nobody manages all of them. At the end you can say only, 'We are unworthy servants; we have only done our duty'" (Luke 17:10).

"Thank you for the faith you have given me so far to finish the 'some'!"

"There will be faith enough to finish the rest," he assured me.

I thought about the sense of "sent-ness" I had experienced as I had gone about my daily doings because God had invested the minor duties with major meaning. Knowing and loving him had not only brought me fulfillment but also had given me a driving determination to accomplish the most mundane tasks properly whether anyone was looking or not!

Before I knew the Lord, I had always had to have an audience. Because I craved attention and affirmation, I didn't bother to work hard or behave properly if I thought no one was looking. After my conversion I came to understand that you are who you really are in the dark. The most important affirmation is the affirmation that comes from God (who sees right through the dark anyway) for the darkness and the light are both alike to him: "If I say, 'Surely the darkness will hide me and the light become night around me,' even the darkness will not be dark to you; the night will shine like the day, for darkness is as light to you" (Psalm 139:11-12). It was that all-important audience of One that I had to care about. Jeremiah had taught me that lesson. He had to draw his affirmation from God alone most of the time. He was accountable to God alone for who he was both in the light and in the dark.

"Lord," I said, "I want those who know you to get a conscious sense of destiny about their choices and decisions along life's way. It's good when we realize that it's 'your work in our hands.'" I thought awhile about the times I had said eagerly and breathlessly on my knees, "How could something as mundane as this be so much fun!" I knew the answer to the *how* of course. It all depended on making sure *where* I was truly living—was I on the salt flats or on the riverbank? "I love that parable, Lord," I said.

"It's such a good picture," the Lord agreed. "There is no need to be a withered little scrub bush when you can be an evergreen tree. Along the rest of the way, keep putting out your roots by my river of life. Life in the Spirit necessitates that you draw on my power and be refreshed by the living water."

I thanked him then for his Holy Spirit and for promising to be the enabling of all that he asks of us in the grander scheme of things. For appointing, assisting, and anointing us to face the faces of those to whom he sends us.

There will be enough faces to intimidate us, enough circumstances to discourage us, enough opposition to tempt us to trim our message of judgment and grace, and enough insecurity for us to protest, with Jeremiah, "I do not know how to speak; I am only a child!"

To all of this whining, God will calmly reply, as he has in the past, "Do not say, 'I am only a child [or an old lady].' You must go to everyone I send you to and say whatever I command you. . . . I have put my words in your mouth." Calling, commissioning, and communicating will busy us with kingdom work and fulfill us. Our part will be to do the mind work. God's part will be to do the heart work. As we are careful to mind our minds as God minds our hearts, the work will be accomplished. If things are right when we are on our knees, they will be right when we are on our feet.

If and when we come unstuck and start to get God and life mixed up, his compassions will never fail. They will be "new every morning," and great will be his faithfulness.

"Even when our companions are driving us crazy, Lord, and we are finding it difficult to keep on course because you have put some difficult people in our lives, you will help us. With your guidance we can find some common ground, celebrate the differences, and understand the why of their behavior. You have done it before, and you will do it again. We will try, O God, to say, 'You choose my team,' and mean it!"

"Don't forget Jeremiah and Baruch, Jill," he reminded me. "It wasn't easy for them. They did it, and did it again and again, and they did it together."

"Doing things again is hard, Lord. The older I get the more I try to get by with the mediocre. I'm tempted to edit the manuscript once instead of twice and to prepare 'old' talks instead of new material. Help me to remember that your name is 'Excellent,' so that I will try to do 'excellent' work for you."

"I will," he promised.

"And about this chisel, Lord," I began, but he stopped me.

"Shall the sculpture say to the sculptor, 'Why have you made me so?' "

Then I put my hand over my mouth and put my face in the dust. I knew there was no other way, and I would feel the *chip, chip, chip* of the chisel until the day I walked through the Front Door. But I also knew that the hands that held the chisel were nail pierced and tender and that the work in progress that was "me" would continue because he loved me to death. And in loving me to death, he had loved me to life!

"Shape us then, oh Lord, shape us. Chisel the David out of us to your great glory. And when we seek great things for ourselves, speak sternly to our hearts. Point out our pride and ambition and put us on our faces where we belong. May we stop whining and say with spiritual abandon, 'Lay it on us, Lord, lay it on us!' Break our hearts, God. May your tears be on our faces and your hurt be in our hearts. There is no other way, is there, Lord? If there were, you would have told us!"

Above all, I have learned all over again through this study that tears are a language all their own. And I have learned that I am becoming a little bit more like the Master when I cry not for myself but for him. So I spent some time thinking about this as I readied this book for publishing, thanking the Lord that when I am lost for words, I know through my friend Jeremiah that my tears talk. That they knock on the Front Door and are always admitted to the throne room any time of the day and night. Above all, I know, with a huge sense of gratitude, that moment by moment, day by daily day, yoke by yoke, crisis by crisis, because his compassions never fail and because great is his unfailing love—*I am heard!*

I Am Heard

Tears talking,
Pattering petition on the door of heaven,
Let me in.
Wet misery,
Fountains of fury,
Rivers of recriminations,
Tears tearing down the riverbed of doubt,
Stopping at the throne.
Bottled bereavement
Arranged by angels,
Given to the King.

God tilts the bottle carefully over his book onto a clean page.
Transported in a teardrop,
Translated into eloquence,
My washing woe writes its words of wounded worry down.
Splashing sadness signs its name;
Then dry depression comes to stay for all the tears have gone.

The Father reads my tears
And passes the book to the Son,
Who shares it with the Spirit.

The angels gather round.
Some small celestial cherubs are lifted to the Father's knee,
The story is told;
They listen, they all listen.
I am heard!

"I have heard her prayers, I have seen her tears," says the Father.
"I am touched with the depth of her sorrow," says the Son.
"I will pray for her with groanings that cannot be uttered,"
    says the Spirit.
"And God will wipe away all tears from her eyes," sing the angels.
"And there shall be no more death,

Neither sorrow nor crying,
Neither shall there be any more pain,
For the former things are passed away."

Tears talking,
Pattering petition on the door of heaven,
Let me in.
They listen, they all listen,
I am heard!

Other Books by Jill Briscoe

Heartstrings
Daily Study Bible for Women
Prayer That Works
One Year Book of Devotions for Women

About the Author

Jill Briscoe's active speaking and writing ministry has taken her to many countries. She is the author (or coauthor) of more than forty books, including devotional material, poetry, study guides, and children's books. Jill is the executive director of *Just Between Us*, a magazine providing encouragement to ministry wives and women in leadership. She also serves on the board of directors for World Relief and for Christianity Today International.

A native of Liverpool, England, Jill began working in youth evangelism after becoming a Christian at age eighteen. She and her husband, Stuart, were married in 1958, and since that time they have ministered together through Telling the Truth media ministries at conferences and missions organizations around the world.

Jill and Stuart live in suburban Milwaukee, Wisconsin, where Stuart has just completed thirty years of ministry as senior pastor of Elmbrook Church. Both Stuart and Jill now serve Elmbrook as ministers-at-large. They have three grown children, David, Judy, and Peter, and enjoy the blessing of thirteen grandchildren.

Faith Enough to Finish
has companion audio and video tapes.

To order these and other books, tapes, and videos
by Jill or Stuart Briscoe,
call 1-800-248-7884,
or visit **www.tellingthetruth.org**

For more information about *Just Between Us,*
a magazine of encouragement for ministry
wives and women in leadership,
call 1-800-260-3342, or
visit **www.justbetweenus.org**